I0003241

Dynamic Customer Strategy

Dynamic Customer Strategy

Today's CRM

John F. Tanner, Jr.

Dynamic Customer Strategy: Today's CRM
Copyright © Business Expert Press, LLC, 2014.
All rights reserved. No part of this publication may be reproduced,
stored in a retrieval system, or transmitted in any form or by any
means—electronic, mechanical, photocopy, recording, or any other
except for brief quotations, not to exceed 400 words, without the prior
permission of the publisher.

First published in 2014 by
Business Expert Press, LLC
222 East 46th Street, New York, NY 10017
www.businessexpertpress.com

ISBN-13: 978-1-60649-696-1 (paperback)
ISBN-13: 978-1-60649-697-8 (e-book)

Business Expert Press Marketing Strategy Collection

Collection ISSN: 2150-9654 (print)
Collection ISSN: 2150-9662 (electronic)

Cover and interior design by Exeter Premedia Services Private Ltd.,
Chennai, India

First edition: 2014

10 9 8 7 6 5 4 3 2 1

Printed in the United States of America.

Abstract

Marketers, merchandisers, and sales executives alike are struggling with Big Data—the data streaming at increasing speeds from myriad channels and options for communicating with customers. The tools are likely to continue to multiply, paralyzing many executives with simply too many choices. Using data from a four-year study, this book provides a process for rigorous decision making, eliminating the paralysis and optimizing decision making for marketing performance.

This book is intended for a broad audience including students and professors in graduate business schools, and practicing business executives. The goal is to inform marketing practice and help current and future business leaders navigate through the competitive storms unleashed by technological change.

Keywords

big data, customer relationship management, customer strategy, omnichannel marketing, multichannel marketing, shopper journey, path to purchase, attribution modeling, dynamic customer strategy, integrated marketing management, marketing automation

Contents

CHAPTER 1

Big Data and Dynamic Customer Strategy

The only sustainable competitive advantage
is the ability to learn faster than your competition,
and to be able to act on that learning.
—Jack Welch, former CEO, GE

Introduction

This book is written for two audiences: Business executives who want to understand what big data will mean for their business and how they create strategies; and business students who need to learn how marketing strategy is planned in the more successful organizations. This chapter addresses the following questions:

- What is big data and how will it change strategy?
- What is Dynamic Customer Strategy?
- Do I have to throw out all I know about strategy and start over?

In today's turbulent marketplace, it seems like a new channel to reach customers is introduced every day. Data is piling up at an ever-increasing rate with over 2.5 quintillion bytes per day.

Just consider Black Friday and Cyber Monday—the two biggest shopping days of the year for most retailers, and the two days that can mean the difference between a good year and a bad year. Every one of those transactions generates data. Every transaction carries a data trail that actually extends back perhaps weeks. Every abandoned shopping cart contains valuable information. There's every website the shopper visited, whether the purchase was made in-store or online. There's every forum, every community site, every call center interaction all lined up behind that transaction. It's no wonder, then, that by 2015 the amount of data companies store will double, and by 2020, it will double two more times!

That's Big Data: data at an increasing rate of Volume, Variety, and Velocity.[1]

Does Big Data matter? If you aren't excited about this topic already consider this: McKinsey Global Institute estimates that we're 1.5 million short of the number of data-capable managers needed.

If it takes you six days to compile all of that data, analyze it, and get interpretable results to a merchandiser, then you've lost four days of marketing effort to your competitors. Or maybe six days.

What you should learn here is how to manage Big Data for big profits. As a data-capable leader, you'll be the one who turns that data into decisions: What to offer Norman who abandoned a cart or what to place in front of Norma after she left your website. Getting your systems into shape to take advantage of such data is a must in today's Big Data world.

But wait, that's only part of the story. How do those predictive models get built in the first place? What matters to Norman and what's different about Norma? And how can we get them both to purchase without having to offer a discount? That's the strategy part—that's the part that separates those who swim through Big Data and those who drown in it. And that is the purpose of this book—to help you swim through Big Data.

Introducing Dynamic Customer Strategy

For a little more than a decade, a few scholars and practitioners have been exploring a new approach, a new way to consider data and strategy. I've been speaking and writing on the subject, mainly to deaf ears because the concepts have seemed so foreign to the way we've thought about strategy. In addition, this new approach does require some analytical ability, and a lot of really creative people shy away from anything smacking of analytics.

This new approach to strategy is called Dynamic Customer Strategy (DCS). We call it Dynamic Customer Strategy because when applied, organizations are free from those practices that locked them into strategies even while the market changed. We call it Dynamic Customer Strategy because innovation becomes the modus operandi, the way of doing things.

Sounds great, doesn't it! But first, a brief history lesson, and not just for the sake of academic interest. This history lesson is presented because you'll see how organizations have been trapped by the limits of their tools.

The Dawn of Strategy

You might think that Harvard was the first school to offer the study of business. After all, Harvard's cases are synonymous with MBA and strategy. But actually, Harvard wasn't the first US school to offer students the opportunity to study business; that distinction belongs to Wharton. Harvard wasn't even the second. But what Harvard, besides being the first to offer the MBA, is where the case method of teaching originated. They started the case method because in 1910, when they began offering the MBA, there were no textbooks in business. There were textbooks in economics dating back to the mid-1800s, but none on the various ways of doing business.

The case method of teaching, especially at the beginning when there wasn't a body of knowledge against which to judge whether the actors in the case were doing the right things, simply became a way of presenting business problems and teaching students how to solve them. Then, as faculty began applying scientific methods to the study of business, the body of knowledge was built up and layered on to the case discussions. Students began to apply tools like the Boston Consulting Group (BCG) grid (source), Porter's Five Forces (source), and others.

The case method has been pretty successful in preparing business managers with solid technical and problem-solving skills. But the case method also led to the notion that somehow strategy was more important than tactics, that thinking was better than doing, and that these could be separated and so that the thinking could be done by consultants and the doing by management.

When I began my business career, I actually worked on a strategy team. True, I was nothing more than a research grunt, providing analyses of the financial strength and strategies of our customers and our competitors. My work contributed to strategic decisions like ending our Telex business and moving toward markets comprised of customers like MCI (Sprint's predecessor) and others. Yet, no one on our team actually had any operating business responsibility. That was 1977, perhaps the height of the Design School of strategy, which is the approach that resulted from Harvard's case-teaching method and was based on the belief that strategy is one activity, implementation another.

Then along came a Canadian named Henry Mintzberg, who suggested that not only was the MBA stifling the creative development of highly intelligent students and thereby stifling the development of their employers, but that the Design School was not really how strategy was getting done. He wrote that strategy is not separated from execution but emerges from actions, that strategy and implementation are not just two sides of the same coin but so intertwined as to be yin and yang. He called this approach to understanding strategy the Emergent School.

When I was introduced to this radical concept, I began to think, "If this guy is right, what tools do we marketers need to harness the power of Emergent Strategy?" And thus began the research that led to DCS.

Why not stay with calling it Emergent? Because Emergent describes what results from action, whether or not there is any effort on the part of the leader to shape it. No matter whether the firm engages in activities aligned with traditional strategy practices or has no formal strategy, a strategy will emerge from action. Dynamic, on the other hand, not only implies agility and creativity, it also implies control. We were working on a new way to practice strategy, not describe strategy. Emergent, Mintzberg's emphasis, describes what happened; Dynamic describes what should happen.

What is Dynamic Customer Strategy?

As we began to consider what leaders need to take control over strategy, the need for skills in certain areas became obvious: experimental design, data management, statistics, and so forth. This recognition led to discussions with business executives, graduate students, and other faculty on the process of living strategically, resulting in a decade of research devoted to understanding the relative value and the practice of the approach and the tools described in later chapters.

DCS is a skillset and toolset to capture market value through agile marketing. The toolset involves all of those things mentioned above. The practice involves identifying and securing targets of opportunity that contribute to strategic objectives.

Strategy versus Opportunity

Contrast living strategically with how most people direct their lives. Most humans live opportunistically. Have you ever seen something on sale and bought it because it was too good a deal to pass up, only to get it home and wonder why you bought it? That's acting opportunistically, but acting on an opportunity isn't always a bad thing. Seizing an opportunity to introduce yourself to a beautiful woman or handsome man might just lead to the love of your life.

Recently, my son and I invested in a flip house. We had to do significant renovation and when we were done, we barely broke even. When my wife said, "Well, we don't have to do that again," my son replied with, "Yes, we do. That was an expensive education; I don't want to waste it." He saw an opportunity and he took it—but did it make sense strategically? We'll talk more about this later in the book—about how to distinguish between good opportunities and strategic opportunities because the real challenge isn't always distinguishing between good and bad investments. The real challenge lies in separating the good opportunities from the strategic opportunities.

DCS isn't about being only opportunistic. The DCS-based firm is opportunistic in ways that contribute to strategic objectives.

Applying Dynamic Customer Strategy

In a nutshell, DCS can be described like this:

1. Everyone does things because they see a relationship between the action, the outcome, and the reward. On the macro-scale of a company, the relationship between action, outcome, and reward is influenced by other factors, sometimes a lot of factors.

2. With DCS, you identify and define as many of the factors as you can, their effects on actions and outcomes, and the amount of control you have over them.

3. Your actions, then, become experiments as you test whether the relationships between these factors operate as you hypothesized.

4. Now, with sophisticated information technology, you can collect the data and impose sufficient control over the process to benefit from DCS. As a result, you can test far more scenarios simultaneously (not just 2 versions of the same message, for example, as in A/B testing but as many as 25 versions of 25 messages). You learn faster because you can cycle through more tests, and as you learn, you change your model.

DCS puts into practice one of my favorite quotes, the one which opened this chapter and is attributed to Jack Welch, former CEO of GE and founder of his own school of business, which is now part of Strayer University. He said, "The only sustainable competitive advantage is the ability to learn faster than your competition, and to be able to act on that learning."

That's the beauty of DCS. If you look back at the four elements listed earlier, you can see that what DCS offers is a way to increase the velocity of organizational learning, while at the same time increasing the velocity of acting on that learning.

These two dimensions are the heart of DCS: the velocity of learning and the velocity of action. By speeding up the flywheel for both, we accelerate all manner of business cycles. Product development can be ramped up and amped up because we'll learn consumer reactions that much faster. Channel choices can be altered quickly, and the relative investment shifted to where it will do the most good. Pricing is optimized, with yield pricing models influencing demand rather than the other way around.

As the velocity of the two dimensions of learning and action increase, failure occurs more quickly, a good thing because quick failure reduces investment risk while minimizing opportunity risk. Investment risk is reduced because we don't continue to sink resources into what will ultimately (or quickly) fail. Opportunity risk is minimized because we're able to find better opportunities more rapidly.

The velocity of learning and the velocity of action have two important payoffs. The first is illustrated in Exhibit 1.1; the ability to learn and act more quickly creates the opportunity to derive more value from a relationship with a customer. If we can respond to a customer event more quickly, we can capture more business. For example, if we can identify a customer's web browsing pathway and link it to known purchase opportunities, we can then respond with an offer that increases the likelihood of purchase from us. Otherwise, that customer may continue along that web browsing path to another vendor, another time, another channel.

To achieve this increased velocity, we have to have faster data acquisition tools, analysis models that are automatic, and response mechanisms that are tied to the automated models, and be able to offer strategies that respond to the immediate needs of our buyer. When we put all of these together, we have a dynamic system (dynamic because it responds to the individual needs of the consumer) that operates with greater velocity.

What you see in Exhibit 1.1 is increased operational velocity. The value of increased learning velocity is illustrated in Exhibit 1.2. Using a new product design as an example, Mitsubishi's heating and air conditioning business claims a two year advantage over competitors because of their ability to learn and respond to the market more quickly (coupled with an ability to design more quickly). In financial markets, Egg (a former standalone bank purchased by Citi) was able to design new products and services in less than 6 weeks, compared to the industry standard of 6 months to a year, a competitive advantage entirely attributed to their ability to learn what the market wanted faster.

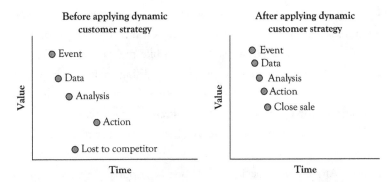

Exhibit 1.1. Currently, most organizations follow the pattern on the left—by the time someone recognizes that an opportunity is there, the consumer purchased from someone else. Accelerate the event to action cycle and you increase the probability of making the sale, and the value is greater for both parties.

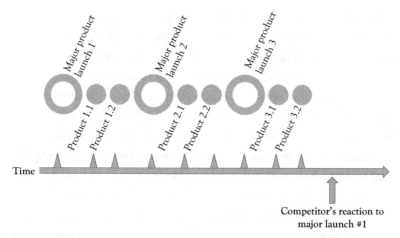

Exhibit 1.2. Value of faster learning in new product design.

Source: Adapted from Dwyer and Tanner (1999).

When you recall that Big Data is big because of volume, variety, and *velocity*, then the relationship between DCS and Big Data becomes more apparent. Without the toolset of DCS, taming Big Data isn't possible.

Benefits of Dynamic Customer Strategy

As already noted one important benefit of implementing a DCS approach is taming Big Data. Other benefits also accrue. One desirable outcome of DCS is a common language because we defined what the terms mean in our business. We all think we speak the same language in our organizations, but stop for a moment. Who is a loyal customer? Is it someone who has signed up for the loyalty program? Or is it someone who, in the immortal words of Sally Fields, says "you like me, you really like me." You may have your definition, the merchandising managers have their definition, and senior execs have yet another. It's no wonder that those execs shake their heads at some of the strategies they see—they ask for one thing and get something entirely different. But the mismatch is not because of ineptitude, it is because the message sent is not the message received. Any match is accidental, it isn't intentional, because the same words had different meanings. When DCS is applied properly, one common language results for the organization.

That one language is nearly impossible with the Design School, or at least, it certainly rarely occurred, because of the distance between the thinkers and doers. When I was a sales rep for Xerox, I was asked to train PIP sales reps on my sales process. PIP sales reps were those on Performance Improvement Probation, in other words 90 days to get your sales up or get a new job. I asked them how many prospects each had. The answer ranged from 20 plus to over 30, certainly many more than I ever had at one time (our sales quota only required four sales per month). I quickly realized, however, that what these reps were calling a prospect was someone who had a very low probability of purchasing. Further, they carried these prospect lists around like a security blanket for months, yet the decision cycle was typically less than two weeks. Any prospect that lasted longer than two weeks really wasn't a prospect because they weren't going to buy anytime soon. But more importantly, our different definitions of what is truly a prospect were leading to differences in activity and that led to the difference in our performance. If you have a lot of prospects, you don't do much prospecting. I always had few prospects, so I was always looking for more. PIP reps, on the other hand, were browbeating people who had no reason to buy, angering their "prospects," and draining themselves of emotional capital when they should have been looking for real prospects.

Couldn't we have just come up with a common definition and ensured everyone would be happy? Sure, we could and we did–at our local level. But because strategy was planned in Rochester, New York and I sold in Dallas, my definition of prospect was no more the same as a rep's in LA. "So what?" you ask. I'll tell you, my sales cycle needed to be a function of the organization's strategy, tied in with advertising, trade shows, direct mail, and all the channels of that time. Nowadays, my sales cycle should reflect the company's web browsing data capture definitions, the social customer relationship management (CRM) strategy, and so forth. If someone sends me a lead, I better have a good understanding of what that lead represents, where it is in the sales cycle, the probability of closing, and so forth. If my definition is off, I'll do the wrong thing, which could include doing nothing and wasting all that marketing effort.

No, this doesn't mean, as one student thought, that you control language through DCS. It's just that one result of DCS is the shared meaning of what various but very important terms mean. Like customer. (How long does someone have to not buy before he can no longer be considered a customer?)

DCS does more than allow you to come up with a common language; it also helps you develop an organization-wide understanding of strategy. That means that everyone is pulling in the same direction. The Design School left that "let's all head here" to the mission statement. But that left a lot to be determined at the local level which meant that a great deal of corporate effort was wasted. With DCS, operational units are far more likely to understand roles, obligations, and action plans.

Case Study

Cabela's is the World's Foremost Outfitter, meaning they serve the needs of those who enjoy the outdoors. Their customers are hikers, campers, those who like to fish or hunt, bird watchers, and others who participate in woodsy or marine activities.

Over the past five years (July 2008 to 2013), the company's stock has grown from about $11.50 per share to almost $70, significantly outperforming the rest of the market. Keep in mind, that includes the Great Recession, a time in which Cabela's did lose half its value, but by the end of 2009, the company had improved on that 2008 value by 50%, and has since sky-rocketed in value. How?

In large part, this company's growth epitomizes what is possible with DCS. One particular example stands out, a project I worked on that began for me in July, 2010.

The company was changing vendors for capturing web-browsing data, that is, the software that tracks your movement when you are on a website. I was given the opportunity to document that change and how it would help marketing as a case study. In the process, though, I learned that Cabela's shoppers were loading up their cart on the web but then sometimes abandoning it several times before buying. Not all shoppers, but enough to show an emerging pattern that was troubling because these shoppers didn't always come back and buy. Important to note is that Cabela's has the ability to track customer purchases no matter what channel—in-store, via the web, from a catalog, etc. And they can do this for greater than 80% of the purchases that take place, which is a very high rate of customer identification.

Over the course of the next few months, we discussed that concern and I suggested that maybe the issue was simply that the buyer didn't see enough value to go through the hassle of checking out. Maybe instead of worrying about what led someone to abandon a basket, we look at what constitutes enough value to buy. This led to an exploration of the order in which items are placed in the basket so that we could identify those products of sufficiently high value (to the customer) that would lead to a sale. We then identified a group of products that we labeled "basket-starters" (I know, not very clever) because the probability of purchasing was much higher if they went in the basket first.

Cabela's then created an email campaign that led with a basket-starter, a different one depending on the type of customer. A customer who fishes got a fishing offer, a hunter got a hunting offer, etc. Then, they ran the campaign while running a huge discount promotion to another group of the same types of customers. What was interesting is that the basket-starter outperformed the big discount offer, even though there was no discount given on the basket-starter. Since then, we've run similar campaigns with similar results.

Two things stand out about this example. First is the process. Note that Cabela's took data, learned from it, acted on it, and created an offer that was of high value to both Cabela's and the customer. This process of *learn, test, learn, act* defines the Cabela's culture and exemplifies DCS. Second is the data. Without the ability to integrate data across all sources and all channels, we would never have been able to identify basket-starters with the same precision. Nor would we have been able to then multiply the value of that learning by repeating basket-starter offers on a regular basis. None of this would have been possible without DCS.

No More Design School?

If Mintzberg developed his thinking about the MBA and emergent strategy in response to what he saw as shortcomings in the Harvard-style MBA, does that mean that Design School strategy is wrong? That we don't need to do strengths/weaknesses-opportunities/threats (SWOT) analyses anymore or that Porter's Five Forces might be three or six, and who cares because it's irrelevant anyway? Is the demise of Porter's own consulting company evidence that the Design School is wrong?

No, not in the least.

Let's look, for a moment, at how the traditional work of strategy gets done. Starting in September, executives and managers start planning for the next year. This set of activities is called *strategic planning*. There may be an executive retreat where much drinking, golf, and navel gazing takes place, but most of the work is done in tediously long and boring meetings, with a review of last year's plan resulting in an adjustment and the new plan.

Then, assuming that no crisis looms, threatening to destroy the world as we know it, every five to ten years (or more often, when a new CEO is named), the Board reviews the company's mission statement. Consultants are brought in to take the leadership team through some sort of strategic planning process. A notebook is created, documenting both the process and the new strategy, and then it is shelved next to the old one and life goes on.

Sounds familiar? I know I'm guilty—I've even led facilitations of leadership teams through such a process. We used tools like SWOT and portfolio matrices like the BCG grid to develop a strategy.

But these weren't bad toolkits, they were just incomplete. The result of these types of processes is simply the starting point for DCS.

So don't throw out everything you've ever known about how to create strategy. I'm not saying your MBA wasn't worthwhile. Or that your business is doomed unless you swallow this new magic pill, stuff this new silver bullet into your revolver, or follow this new path to salvation. There are a lot of good businesses that got good without DCS, and you can be one of those if you wish. Just not as good. And maybe not as long-lasting.

Why Now? What's Different Now?

Yes, the world is changing and how business gets done is changing rapidly. As I said earlier, it seems a new marketing channel is being born every day. Moreover, consumers are migrating from one to the next faster than marketers can keep up.

Just think, today there are more tweets than people (Source). And Twitter is only one of the new channels; thinks of Pinterest, Facebook, and all of the others. The story of chaotic channel proliferation is both staggering and well-known. The impact on business has been nothing short of terrific. Companies hired over 180,000 people by the end of 2011 just for handling marketing through Facebook.[2]

Another well-known but also staggering story is that of data and the information explosion. We only thought that data exploded a decade ago. Now we have the ability to scrape web browsing behavior, measure the influence of individual consumers, map their social networks, and a host of other activities. What's important is to also recognize that these uses of data also create data–a Klout score of your online influence, for example, may be a representation of dozens of variables but it is also a variable. What data must we have and what will we do with it? And what does that have to do with DCS? The answer to that is in the chapter on data strategy. For now, though, recognize that new data sources continue to proliferate, and they are not all equally valuable.

Technology, thankfully, has kept up. Enterprise data warehouses, such as those developed by Teradata, have accelerated our ability to store and, more importantly, access data. Statistics software providers like SAS and SPSS not only advance the development of predictive models, they automate some of the modeling techniques. These automated techniques make fairly sophisticated analysis much easier and much more accessible. Of course, there is also the possibility of misapplication, of using a technique incorrectly for the data that are available, but for many users, these icon-based drag-and-drop stats packages can work remarkably well. And all kinds of other technology applications, from mobile to imaging (QCR codes) to even radio frequency identifiers (RFID) make all sorts of channels possible.

More importantly, these technologies add two elements that increase the velocity of strategy and learning. First, they make that elusive 360 degree view of the customer possible. But not just the view of the customer. These same technologies also add information about and across the value network. (Notice I didn't say value chain, it's not linear, but we'll talk more about that later). Second, they add test and control capabilities in a high-velocity real-world environment. Without these two elements, DCS is harder to do. Not impossible. Just harder.

Why Not Now?

If DCS is so great, why isn't everyone implementing it? That's just it, everyone does implement DCS to some extent; or at least, no matter what is done, a strategy will emerge. But there are barriers that act like governors on a truck.

During World War II, and even to this day in some countries, some vehicles were equipped with a governor, an apparatus that limits the vehicle's speed. Created to force drivers to maintain a speed that conserved fuel, these are now used to improve road safety, support union rules on work hours, and so forth.

In spite of our natural tendency to think and operate in a dynamic fashion, there are governors, or barriers, on our ability to make full use of the DCS approach. Some barriers operate at the individual level; that is, these barriers inhibit us as individuals in carrying out a dynamic approach. Others operate at the organizational level and really simply reflect individual barriers thrown up at the organizational level.

One barrier, though, is Big Data. As data grows in volume, variety, and velocity, data systems are overwhelmed. Fortunately, new technologies are overcoming this barrier. Further, Big Data are not required for DCS, though Big Data requires a Dynamic approach.

We've found in our research that the biggest barrier is simply turf. DCS may be applied to campaign management in marketing, as we observed in one company, but when leads are tossed over the transom to sales, they enter a black hole with no feedback at all. Clearly, without the ability to close the loop and know what ultimately happened with each lead, the learning that could be used to improve the lead management cycle has been lost. In sales force-dominant organizations (organizations we define as having a sales force as the primary go-to-market channel), arrogance on the part of the sales force and sales leadership separates sales from the rest of the company. When the belief that "I am responsible for my own success" morphs into "I am a sales god and no one can help me perform any better than I do now," one result is a barrier that inhibits the opportunity to practice DCS.

I can hear the salespeople now saying one of two things. First, "I'm not like that!" yet I've seen a salesperson whose performance depended on the pre-sales support of engineers walk into a meeting and toss the keys of his new Mercedes on the table, just to show it off. He gave no thought to the fact that the engineers sitting around the table who were critical to the big sale that paid for the new car got no bonus (shame on the company for that).

True, most salespeople aren't that bad. But how often do your salespeople roll their eyes when marketing comes out with a new lead-generation program? Does anyone bother to follow up on those leads? Or how carefully do the salespeople enter data into the CRM system? Yet those same salespeople mutter and complain about the poor quality of leads they get (and therefore don't follow up) whereas the poor quality may be due to the poor quality of data they entered in the system. And because of that incomplete or inaccurate data, marketing couldn't generate a solid model for **lead scoring** (that is, determining the quality of a lead before giving it to sales).

What about organizations that are not sales force dominant? Where are the barriers there?

Arrogant thinking, complacency, and other human barriers exist in all organizations. Turf is not just a sales versus marketing thing. Before you move on to the other barriers, check yourself. Check your organization. Are there battles over access to data? Do you observe a lack of urgency on the part of someone else keeping you from obtaining the support you need? Do you run into departments, like IT or engineering, that act as though they are the only reason for the firm's success? Toss in a few short-sighted individuals, and you've got turf battles.

Another barrier, though, may not be so obvious, and that's fear. On the part of many marketing and sales types, one limiting fear is the fear of math. DCS does require statistics and few marketing and sales types like math. On the other hand, engineers and accountants are not too sure about marketing and this whole creativity thing. Scott Adams, creator of the comic strip *Dilbert*, once wrote that marketing is just liquor and guessing. Not today. Good strategy needs both creativity and statistics. Going on a gut is ok for a while, but at some point, you have to do the math to know if what your gut told you is right.

The final barrier, at least in terms of commonality across the companies we observed, is simply a lack of commitment. Call it firefighting, quota-busting, or what you will, in some organizations we observed an inability to simply take the time to master the approach. Even organizations that identified a need to do strategy differently, yet were unwilling to commit to making a change have been unable to grow. In one instance, a $10 million dollar company lost its largest customer. Rather than recognizing that strategy was to blame, they decided they had to make up the revenue shortfall by simply running the hamster on the wheel a little faster. The best I think this company can hope for is to be acquired into oblivion, for oblivion is where it is headed.

And Off We Go...

There are, of course, other barriers that can trip up any change. Two factors, though, are worth mentioning.

First, we're not proposing an entirely new approach. Rather, we're documenting the steps that can be taken to make what an organization is already doing more successful. As individuals, we all follow DCS principles; it's just some people do so a little better. We're not asking you to give up chocolate, take up exercise, or any other major life change, just bring a certain discipline to what you are already doing.

Second, while organizations work best when DCS is implemented across an organization, we've observed many companies where DCS is limited to one functional area. In fact, most often the tools and skills are honed in that one functional area or department, migrating from there across the firm. If you're not the CEO, it doesn't matter. You can still implement these tools even in one small area of operations.

Summary

Big Data is characterized by Volume, Variety, and Velocity. It's more data, coming from more sources, and at greater speed. The challenge is to convert that into insight. To do that, we need to understand how the factors represented by the data influence customer lifetime value and other important outcomes. So we create a conceptual model that illustrates the relationships between those variables, and we can use that model to create and test a strategy that is more dynamic, flexible, and adaptive to the changing conditions of the market.

This new approach doesn't replace what you've always known about strategy; rather, this approach can complement what is known as the Design School. But the key is to learn faster than your competition and be able to act on that learning.

Discussion Questions

1. What's the biggest difference between the Design School or Harvard approach to strategy and Dynamic Customer Strategy? What makes that difference so important? Or to put it another way, how does only doing a Design-based strategy create challenges in an organization?

2. How does Big Data make DCS possible? Do you have to have Big Data to make use of DCS, and vice-versa?

3. Of the three Vs of Big Data, which one is the most difficult for organizations to master? Why is that one the most difficult to handle?

CHAPTER 2

The Elements of Dynamic Customer Strategy

All the world is a laboratory to the inquiring mind.
—Martin H. Fischer

Introduction

Dynamic Customer Strategy (DCS) reaches that middle ground between the big vision of the organization and what marketing actions are taken. But to understand the linkage between big strategy and Big Data, we'll first explore the element of DCS. From this chapter, you should be able to:

- Identify the factors that operate in a particular market to influence sales and other outcomes
- Describe the relationships between those factors
- Separate factors that cause outcomes from other factors that may be present and may influence but not cause outcomes

From the moment we are born, we begin to learn how we can influence the world around us. We learn that if we cry, we get attention. If we want food, we cry. If we want a clean diaper, we cry. If we want to be rocked to sleep, we cry.

Much of the rest of our life is then spent figuring out what we want and what we have to do to get it or keep it. As Dave Cronenberg, the movie director, once noted, we're all mad scientists experimenting our way through life. As we experiment, we learn what actually works and what doesn't.

Sometimes, of course, what we think led to success or failure was actually caused by something else. We repeat what we think worked and it doesn't a second time because the real cause wasn't present. Smart people adjust and don't make the same mistake twice. Rather, they search for the true cause.

As we move through life, we develop a number of theories of how things work. If you were at a cocktail party and someone asked, "How should we reduce teen pregnancy?" you could respond with your ideas, based on the observations of your experience, what you have read, and so forth. If you heard a candidate for office describe a plan to "fix" education, you'd evaluate that plan against your theory of what would work. You may not be an expert on either topic, but as you've experienced life, theories on these and many other subjects have developed implicitly in your mind, to be put together on the fly when required.

Strategy is Theory in Use

We all have theories about how things work, and when we develop a strategy, it is based on a particular theory. Few business leaders, however, have studied the subject of theory—what makes for a good theory, how do you know it's a good theory, and the like. Like you, they may have studied theories, such as Porter's Five Forces or Vroom's Expectancy Theory of Motivation or Maslow's Hierarchy of Needs. But have you studied the subject of theory, what makes for a good theory, and how do you know if it is good? Probably not.

Components of a Theory

First, let's examine what makes up a theory. A theory explains the relationship between concepts. For example, satisfaction leads to loyalty, which then leads to customer lifetime value (CLV). Improve satisfaction and loyalty becomes stronger, which then increases CLV. Dissatisfy, and loyalty diminishes, reducing CLV. That is a fairly simple theory.

Conceptual Definitions: In that theory, we have three concepts or variables and two relationships. For this theory to be useful, however, we have to define the concepts. These conceptual definitions specify as clearly as possible what it is we mean when we say loyalty, or satisfaction, or CLV.

You may think you know what loyalty is. If I buy a Diet Coke five times in a row, am I exhibiting loyalty? If I drink water once, am I

Simple model of satisfaction and customer lifetime value

Figure 2.1. This model illustrates the relationship between customer satisfaction, loyalty, and customer lifetime value. As satisfaction improves, loyalty increases which then leads to increased customer lifetime value.

exhibiting disloyalty to Diet Coke? Or do I look loyal if I proclaim to others my unwavering preference for Diet Coke? And what is the difference between habit and loyalty? This latter question is very important, because a good conceptual definition should distinguish clearly between one concept and another.

Loyalty is a good example of the difficulty in defining a concept because there are two types of loyalty: Behavioral and attitudinal. Behavioral loyalty may be exhibited by habitual purchasing over time, whereas attitudinal is a preference for a particular product. As an executive, you may desire behavioral more than attitudinal loyalty because behavioral is the closer of the two concepts to sales, but there is also value in attitudinal loyalty. Attitudinal loyalty is what insulates you against competitive actions, gets you positive word of mouth, and it is what gives you a second chance if you make a mistake. All of those positive consequences should mean more sales and greater CLV.

Why does it matter which loyalty you mean when describing your theory? One reason is that the actions that you take to get behavioral loyalty may be different than those that win you attitudinal loyalty. If you are describing to others in your organization your theory and they take action based on it, they may be earning you the wrong form of loyalty; that is, you may get attitudinal when you wanted behavioral.

A good example is Best Buy. As I write this, pundits are questioning Best Buy's ability to survive. Yet only a few short years before, Best Buy was heralded as the poster child of building loyalty through excellent customer service. But they targeted early adopters of consumer technology, a group which could offer attitudinal loyalty but were notoriously not behaviorally loyal. The company then created compensation plans and metrics that supported transactional purchases in some departments, relationships in others. What happened in the stores was that salespeople operated differently, depending on the department they were in, and consumers got a mixed set of experiences. Yes, there were other problems, but one of the issues they faced was failing to fully define what they wanted, and then failing to communicate that accurately throughout the company.

Creating a clear definition, though, is more than simply avoiding a failure to communicate. Metrics flow from the definition, so success or failure will be measured against the definition. To be sure, communicating the definition is important but it is important to clearly define what it is you want to achieve.

Relationships

As managers, we're not too excited about concepts as stand-alone ideas. Rather, we're interested in **relationships**, or how one variable affects or influences another. Influence is a description of the relationship between one concept and another. For example, one variable could cause another—causality is one form of influence. Clearly specifying the conceptual definition helps minimize the likelihood that you attribute causality incorrectly. We want to repeat those actions that lead to the desired goal and avoid those that fail to achieve the desired objective. But if we attribute a result to an action incorrectly, we will be saddened by failure we can't explain. Or, worse yet, we'll explain away the failure as a function of another cause, and then repeat the action that leads to failure once again. Like the woman married five times who says that all men are bad, we fail to look at ourselves to see if we might be harboring a mistaken view of our own actions.

Conditions

There is another set of variables that we also need to define, and these are our conditions. A **condition** is an environmental variable we can't control. Market volatility, economic stability or instability, inflation or deflation are all variables that describe the conditions in which we operate. For our theory, these conditions influence relationships. In periods of volatility, for example, loyalty might have stronger influence over CLV because loyalty is one way to minimize the potential for the negative impact of the volatility. Or if that volatility is also accompanied by recession, we may see loyalty diminish in power.

Early in my career, the economy went through a period of very high inflation. Annual inflation ran at rates of around 16%, but it varied greatly by product category. Prices for real estate, for example, seemed to be rising at a much faster rate. Anyone, and I do mean anyone, could buy property and sell it two years later at an obscene profit. Compare that experience to the real estate bust of 2008–2012, and you can see that conditions can have a major impact on your ability to predict the future.

Because you can't control conditions, the tendency is to ignore them, at least until they cause a crisis. Recognize the tendency and still think through what the impact of conditions might be. Ok, don't beat yourself up if you didn't see the real estate bust coming; very few of us did. But do consider such factors as changing demographics and what that might mean to your market.

Harley Davidson is the quintessential case study of demographic shift. Their customer base is now in their late fifties to mid-sixties. What happens when these aging motorcyclists can no longer straddle a crotch rocket? You can appeal to that same generation with a motorized tricycle, but eventually too many will need walkers and the market will literally die off. Harley has no control over that condition of changing demographics but they can take action and try to appeal to younger markets. I don't know if they'll go the way of Oldsmobile and other brands that failed to shift their appeal and thus disappeared, but at least Harley saw it coming much sooner and have begun trying to make the shift.

Types of Relationships

By now, you're probably reflecting on your own business and picking out what variables are conditions and which variables are influencing your desired outcomes. You know what makes your business work. You may even be thinking that "I do this already; there's little that's new here."

To some degree, you're right. As I said earlier, you've been practicing some form of DCS since birth.

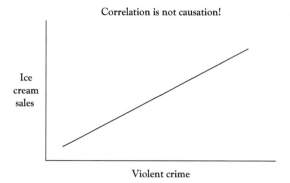

Figure 2.2. Ice cream sales and violent crime are highly correlated, but no one would say crime is caused by ice cream!

Would you like to get better at it?

If so, the real challenge lies in understanding the relationships between variables.

Let's start with an easy one: correlation. A **correlation** is simply an association, meaning that if one variable moves or changes, so does the other. If we plot ice cream sales against violent crime rates, we can see a strong correlation between the two (Exhibit 2.2).

What is it that really causes this relationship? We have correlation, but we don't have causality. For causality, the second type of relationship, we need three things:

1. **Correlation**—when the causal variable changes, so should the outcome variable
2. **Chronology**—the causal variable has to change first; it can't change after the outcome variable
3. **Elimination**—we have to eliminate other possible causes

So what's missing in this instance is elimination; there is likely another variable causing both outcomes. One might think it is the temperature; after all, violent crime and ice cream sales increase in the summer. But there is also a spike in both at Christmas.

What do Christmas and summer have in common? Family gatherings. And most violent crime is perpetrated by a friend or a family member. Both outcomes, in this instance, share the same causal variable, family gatherings.

If you want to promote ice cream sales, promote family gatherings. If you want to promote a reduction in family violence, perhaps promote ice cream as an alternative to alcohol, as alcohol is another factor in family violence.

Another form of relationship is best described in lay terms as an accelerant. If you put a lighter fluid on a fire, it will make the fire burn faster. The lighter fluid doesn't cause the fire—your match does. But the fluid did accelerate the ability of the fire to burn. We have scientific names for these but those are irrelevant. Like alcohol at a family gathering that accelerates the passions that fuel or trigger domestic violence, there are those accelerants in business that can make relationships stronger (or weaker).

Yes, I framed the discussion around accelerants but there are also retardants. They are the same type of variable to scientists because they affect the relationship between two other variables; the only difference being that they slow or inhibit the fire, or they slow or inhibit the purchase.

Causality & Control

We want to know what causes what. Why are our highest value customers not coming in at the same rate? Did we oversell low prices when the economy tanked? Are there simply fewer high value customers out there right now, or what?

All of these are possible causal factors: the economy, our strategy, changes in the make-up of the market. Which is the culprit? Or more likely, how much change is due to which causal factor?

To determine how much each of these factors has influenced our results, and what we should do about it, we have to determine the effect of each. This process is done through eliminating the effects of each causal variable, a process called **control**.

How do you determine the effect of each variable? Since the effect of a variable, such as the economy or dollars spent on advertising, is only recognizable when the causal variable changes, one way to see how much it affects your outcome is to hold the other causal variables constant and change the variable you think has the influence. For example, you could hold prices constant and change how much you spend on advertising. Price and advertising are both thought to be causal variables, but you are seeing what the effect of advertising is by itself. Holding other causes constant and manipulating, or changing, other causal variables is called **experimental control**.

Experimental control makes sense when you can actually control something, and it is what you are doing when you do A/B testing. If you have two advertising campaigns and you randomly select a group of customers to get campaign A and the other group to get campaign B, you are controlling all other causes of difference. It's not the market, it's not the customers, and it's not the competitors because all of those are being held constant, or the same, across the two campaigns.

Keep in mind, though, that the goal is to learn faster than the competition, and to be able to act on that learning (remember our Jack Welch quote). Wouldn't it be nice to be able to test more than just two things at a time?

Of course it would. Overstock.com tests up to 26 variables at a time. Amazon supposedly runs up to 5000 experiments per day. What's the best headline on an email? What's the strongest call to action? When does personalization work—and when does it not? Do men react better to assertive slogans (Nike's "Just Do It") and do women react better to passive slogans (Microsoft's "Where do you want to go today?")? (That study has been done: the answer is it depends more on the product than on the audience's gender.) All of these can be tested simultaneously if you have a good statistician to help you set it up.

But not all variables can be held constant, at least not in real life. You can't hold the economy constant, for example. It will change no matter what you do—you have no control over it. But you can control its effect when your statistician creates a statistical model. This form of control is called **statistical control**. Statistically, procedures can hold the effects of some variables constant if you can't do it experimentally. Also know that you are better off if you can do experimental control, so do so when you can.

Application to DCS

So what does all of this stuff on variables, causality, control, and experiments mean for DCS?

We want to do what works. We want to discover what works. And we want to know that it works.

What is the *what* in "what works?" It is the causal variable. What does "*works*" mean? It is the relationship to the outcome. And how do we know? We prove it by testing. With the discipline of DCS, we can do what works with confidence because we know it works and isn't just some random fluke.

I'm certain some readers are shaking their heads, maybe resting the book in their lap, as they contemplate what they think is an expensive and complicated way to make things more difficult or sell more consulting services. Actually, just the opposite is true.

Yes, you can document the cost of failure. But if you don't know the cause of failure, your costs of failure may be exponentially greater because you'll repeat it.

Even success will vary. Sometimes DCS provides large leaps in progress; other times, simply small steps. The reality is that a few small steps can mean big differences in annual performance whereas large leaps can reshape entire markets.

Even so, what I'm suggesting doesn't have to cost you more to implement. What I am suggesting will cost you more from time to time. ("Aha! Told you so!" say the skeptics.) But, when it does, there should be a documented positive return on investment (ROI).

Case Study: Target

Now that you know that there are causal variables and there are outcomes, held together by relationships and operating in a field of conditions, let's examine how Target puts this DCS stuff to work.

First, the variables.

They wanted behavioral loyalty, or habitual purchasing, and they thought that there might be times when you could interrupt someone's shopping habits and create new ones. For example, when someone moves, new habits are formed. But are there other opportunities?

One might be when a woman becomes pregnant. Their notion was that pregnant women purchase things for the period of being pregnant, and then revert to the original products; the most obvious would be

Target's simple concept map

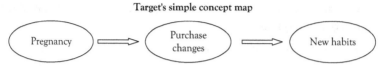

Figure 2.3. Target hypothesized that being pregnant led to changes in certain purchases, which offered opportunities to change shopping habits.

maternity clothes but even that purchase comes later in the pregnancy. What if there were purchases that occurred right away, as soon as she realizes she's pregnant? What would those be?

Their model looks like that illustrated in Figure 2.3.

All of the self-help folks tell us that it only takes about three weeks for a new habit to develop; plenty of time during a pregnancy. But earlier in the pregnancy is better.

To test this model, Target used their database of women who signed up for their Birth Registry for baby showers. These were women who publicly said they were pregnant. Target then examined these women's purchases for a period of 90 days before the registration, and then compared that to another 90 day period well before.

This analysis enabled Target to identify several products, such as unscented hand lotion and vitamins, which signal that a woman knows she is pregnant, even if she hasn't yet registered.

The next step, having identified this product assortment, was to create a marketing campaign that was triggered each time that product assortment occurred. If a woman suddenly began buying vitamins, jeans a size larger, and unscented hand lotion (among other products), the probability was very high that she was pregnant and still in the first trimester. To convert a sometime shopper into a habitual shopper for other products such as grocery items, Target then offered coupons for those pregnancy-related items.

The story doesn't end there. Some women are not ready to publicly announce that they are pregnant, like a certain 16 year old girl in Minnesota. Her father, upset that the store sent her coupons related to pregnancy, called and complained only to call back sheepishly and apologize, as it turned out she was pregnant. That taught Target to be more subtle about the campaign, offering the discounts but as part of a bigger set of offerings that don't signal that Target suspects the pregnancy.

Now, there's a lot to this story, and a lot more to Dynamic Customer Strategy. In the next chapter, we take a look at the data needed to create a DCS.

Summary

In this chapter, the concept of strategy as *theory in use* was presented. Theories represent our view of how the world works, and by explicitly describing those elements we believe impact our results, we craft strategies designed to influence those elements and attain our goals. But in order to determine if those elements truly cause or influence our desired outcomes, we have to ensure that three criteria are met: chronology, correlation, and elimination or control. Control can be accomplished by how we design experiments or through statistics, but the important thing is to eliminate the effects of other variables in order to identify the effects of our actions.

Discussion Questions

1. Assume you work for a university and want to test elements in the school's high school recruiting strategy. Draw out your theory of why students attend that school. How would you use that theory to create a marketing strategy?
2. What's the difference between statistical and experimental control? Give an example of each type of control and why it would be important, using your answer to the first question.
3. Assume the school in question 1 just won a national title in football. You expect that will have an impact on attendance. But what are the underlying causal variables? In other words, why will that have an impact on attendance? Then, use that new model to illustrate causality and correlation by giving examples of other ways to use that same model.

CHAPTER 3

Making Sense of Big Data

The larger the island of knowledge, the longer the shoreline of wonder.
—Ralph W. Sockman

Introduction

Now that we've had an introduction to the elements of Dynamic Customer Strategy (DCS), the need for data is apparent. Not all data are created equal, however. To implement DCS, you must:

- Recognize data traps that can lie within Big Data
- Develop a data strategy.

Data and DCS

DCS requires data. If you want to test your theory of how something works, you need enough data to know. Newton may have figured out gravity after watching one apple fall, but chances are pretty good he had a few data points before that last one hit the ground.

Today's organization has more data than ever before. People have been talking a lot about Big Data and the challenges of managing Big Data, but more data is, by itself, just simply more data not more knowledge.

More than a few years ago, a washing machine manufacturer in India noticed that buyers were ordering eight, 10 or even 20 washing machines but no driers. Who needs a lot of washing machines? Laundromats, prisons, university dormitories, hotels, perhaps, but don't they need driers too? Thinking these buyers were laundromats, the company sent a sales representative to one particularly large customer to offer coin-operated attachments and heavier-duty machines, as well as driers. Imagine the representative's surprise when it was learned these customers were using the machines to make cheese! Yes, cheese! The agitation of the barrels and the top-loaded washing machines were perfect for making a kind of cottage cheese popular in one region of India.

Data is not knowledge. Information is not wisdom. You may think customers are washing clothes when actually, they are making cheese.

Data and Data Traps

Companies need to answer the following questions: How well do you know your best customers? For that matter, how well do you know any of your customers? These are not idle questions, nor are these all the questions that need to be answered but this is a good start.

Most companies, like the washing machine manufacturer, divide their customers into groups based on some measure of value. Depending on the maturity level of the Customer Relationship Management (CRM) program and the experience of those leading it, that value might be gross sales, an index based on profitability estimates, or some other metric. But like the washing machine manufacturer's, this approach is a CRM data trap.

A *data trap* is the illusion of knowing because you have good data—*a lot* of good data. Decision makers think they know a lot about their customer because they have good data on their customer, and this warm, fuzzy feeling of security wraps around their decision making like a baby's blanket. The problem is that the data provide only a limited picture; the rest is filled in with assumptions. "Oh, they must be laundromats." "Oh, all our biggest customers use our product the same way and they all love us." When a company falls prey to a data trap, it makes decisions that seem appropriate for the data that they can get, filling in the missing pieces with assumptions.

Transactional data such as the size of an order creates a data trap because today's enterprise data warehousing technology and Big Data make transactional data easier to access and analyze. Transactional data also adds a layer of information that was previously unavailable, giving marketing professionals more to work with than they ever thought possible. The trap, though, is that so much data from only one source creates an illusion of knowing, rather than actual wisdom.

One fault lies in an assumption that all customers are alike if they purchase the same amount. For example, some companies use Recency, Frequency, and Monetary (RFM) scoring as a proxy for customer lifetime value. RFM Value is a score based on how recently they purchased, how often they purchase, and how big is their average purchase. Like the washing machine company assuming that all multiple machine purchases were intended for laundromats, many companies assume that the drivers for high RFM scores (or heavy use or high volume purchasing) are the same across all high volume purchasers. We say we want one to one marketing, but what we are really saying is we want to talk directly to customers one at a time. Yet, what's difficult to remember, and to operationalize, is that each customer is different, to some degree, and we need to find ways to capture and act on that difference.

Traditional Data Trap

Transactional data is not the only data that creates a data trap. For example, what type of householder would cook all meals in microwaves, owning top-of-the-line units with browning elements? Or have two dishwashers, one for dirty and one for clean dishes? Most people think such a person is likely to be a young professional or a working mother, someone without a lot of time. The first kitchen I saw like that, though, was created by my 80-plus-year-old grandmother—not to save time, but because it was easier on her to not have to unload a dishwasher or slave over a hot stove. But most marketers would assume incorrectly that, because of her age, she was a technophobe rather than an innovator.

Demographic data can also create a data trap. CRM professionals fall into a transactional data trap; traditional marketers fall into a demographic data trap. Traditional marketers tend to treat all members of a demographic group as being the same, whereas many CRM professionals treat all members of a RFM decile (that is, a band of 10% of customers based on RFM score) the same. Victims of either trap are not practicing relationship marketing. What they are doing is using the knowledge they have available to create an illusion of knowing, an illusion that makes them feel like they know their market when, in fact, the actions they take are based on incomplete pictures.

Think of it this way. If you reviewed a million pictures of an elephant's butt, you'd still not have any indication that there was a trunk on the other end. If you have a million transactions to review, you can't tell who's washing clothes and who's making cheese.

Avoiding the Data Trap

Is transactional data not necessary? Does all demographic data lead to the illusion of knowing? Of course not—both transactional and demographic data are needed. Transactional data can help you identify event-based opportunities for dialogue or sales, aid in determining the value of a particular customer or provide insight for other activities. With demographic data, offers can be couched in the right language, and other decisions are supported. But these two forms of data are only a part of the total picture.

The question then becomes how to avoid the data trap—or rather, what is the right blend of transactional, psycho-demographic, and motivational data needed to truly understand the customer? To know the answer to that is to develop a data strategy.

Developing a Data Strategy

A data strategy has four steps:

1. Acquire—find the right data based on the decision to be made or other business need
2. Analyze—develop the right model to inform the decision maker
3. Apply—use the model in making the decision, implementing a strategy, or executing a campaign
4. Assess—review the results to determine if the data and model were worthwhile.

There are two business needs for data. The first is to make a decision now, whereas the second is to simply understand. Clearly, the need to understand will lead to decisions, but I separate the two because understanding is what supports the development of the types of theories that serve the creation of strategy.

First, let's talk about the types of data you need to collect. Big Data is not just more of the same—it's new sources of data, too, many of which were not set up to be data. There's behavioral data, such as web browsing activity; transactional data, such as what was purchased and in what sequence (and academically-speaking, a form of behavioral data); psycho-demographic data which helps us understand lifestyles, age and gender effects, and the like and are heavily used in understanding and promoting brands; and motivational data, or the types of data that help us understand how our buyers consume or use our products. Motivational and psycho-demographic data are very much related; motivational data is specific to the product and use situation but driven by psycho-demographics. Add in descriptive data like blog content, Facebook post content, and the like, and you can see how Big Data is comprised of so many sources of data.

You already know that you need more than just transactional data or you fall into a data trap like the appliance company. Let's take a look at more examples.

Overstock.com's Chief Executive Officer, Patrick Byrne, believes in the value of transactional data because it is behavioral data. He says that you can use that behavioral history to transform future behavior, and he's right. For example, if you can't get some buyers to come back and make a purchase within a certain window, they are lost forever. For Overstock. com, that window is 45 days after their first purchase. At first, Byrne suggested you make a discounted offer to them on the 44th day. The trouble is that not everyone will reply because they weren't there for the discount to begin with, so you aren't offering a relevant message. Another result could be that you are training discount-oriented buyers to wait 44 days, or it could be that you only get price-sensitive buyers to return, losing the higher value customers willing to pay full price.

Every company trains its customers, sometimes unintentionally. For example, Penney trained their buyers to never buy anything at full price by having so many items on sale so often. Customers knew that at least twice a month, many products were drastically reduced, so they waited for the markdowns. In late 2011, JC Penney hired former Apple exec Ron Johnson to turn things around. His first strategy was to wean buyers off of discounts and coupons, trying to give shoppers other reasons to visit Penney.

Unfortunately, he was unable to retrain Penney customers and his tenure was relatively short-lived (about nine months). JC Penney is a cautionary tale for those who use discounts as the first marketing weapon of choice.

Assume Overstock.com had two types of buyers—those who were hard-core discount buyers and those who bought because just because shopping at Overstock was fun. How would this knowledge help them? One way it would help is less reliance on deep discounting. Under Byrne's original thinking, Overstock.com would not necessarily know which type of new customer they were dealing with until the 44th day and a discount was offered. Either the buyer responded to the discount and bought or the discount was ignored. If the buyer does purchase with the discount, perhaps it is a deal-seeking buyer whereas the "fun-seeking" buyer was lost. Only the low-margin customers were retained.

One alternative would be an offer of some fun items or a promotion that appeals to fun-seekers on the 34th day. Ten days later, all non-responders get the discount offer. Now Overstock.com would know who the fun-seekers are and who the hard-core discount buyers are (see Figure 3.1). Future offers could then be tailored to fit the drivers of their behavior. Further, if a large group did not reply to either offer, then perhaps a third group of buyers is appearing. Overstock.com needs to do something to identify what motivates those buyers—and, therefore, needs more data.

	Original *trapped* approach	Dynamic customer strategy approach
Objective	Retain customers	Retain *best* customers
Action	Discount offer on the 44th day	"Fun" offer on 34th day Discount offer on 44th day
Result	Price-sensitive buyers accept offer and shop again	Fun-buyers accept first offer; Price-sensitive customers accept second offer
Outcome	Train customer to wait for discounts	Retains lower-margin buyers; Identifies and retains different buyer groups

Figure 3.1. *Approaches for retaining customers.*

Think back to Chapter 2—you can see that you have two competing theories operating here for why buyers buy. One theory is that buyers shop at Overstock for the bargains; another theory is that they shop there to find unique things because it is fun. The truth is that both could be right, just not right for the same buyers or for the same product categories or for the same situations.

What Data?

To determine what drives or motivates a particular segment, two key areas of data are also needed in addition to transactional and demographic data. These additional types of data are motivational data and lifestyle data. These two types of data are intertwined at the acquisition, the analysis and the application stages. In some situations, motivational or lifestyle data may fall into the "nice to know" category, but consider my grandmother once more. Why hasn't anyone sold a side-by-side dual dishwasher that accomplishes the same thing? Would GE or another company create a market if they understood the people living lifestyles that would benefit from such a product?

Basic CRM promises, such as making an offer individualized to a customer, cannot be fulfilled without motivational and lifestyle data. Even some of the most basic CRM foundations, such as determining your customer's value, are suspect with only transactional or demographic data.

For example, assume you own a fashion retailing firm targeting young women. Reaching them through catalogs, stores, emails, and websites, you have that omnichannel approach down. One question haunts you, though: What is the "life" of your customer? If she is 20 years old, is her customer life another 3 years, 5 years, or 80 years? And can she then be moved into another customer category reached through another division of your company?

Rather than lifetime customer value, perhaps it is better to think about defined customer value. Defined customer value is the value of a customer for a defined product category for a defined period of time. And these definitions also require motivational and lifestyle data.

Earlier, I said that a data trap of any kind is any situation in which you have a lot of data, and it is the volume of data that gives you the illusion of knowing. Some have argued, for example, that the sum of a customer's total transactions over time, multiplied by some expectation of life span, provides a good picture of that person's lifetime value.

Assuming no major changes in the market or innovations alter the relative value, and further assuming the buyer only buys from one company, that could be an acceptable level of knowledge. But it ignores the **share of wallet**, or your share of purchases that the buyer makes out of the budget for that type of purchase. Share of wallet seems easy to calculate, but the key is how big that wallet is.

To really have an idea of a customer's potential value, you have to know what the total purchases are in that category of the buyer's budget. Soft drinks, water, sports energy drinks, and beer are all beverages, but the buyer may not consider those equally as substitutes. Although I've played soccer with guys who think beer is a sports drink, most of us would not consider beer an alternative to PowerAde.

That means understanding *when* the buyer considers your product, and against *which* competitive products is it important to calculate your share of wallet. How the customer calculates the wallet is more important—you may think you compete against energy drinks, for example, but if the customer doesn't consider your beverage when quenching a need for energy, then energy drinks aren't your direct competition.

Here's another aspect to consider: time. How much time does your buyer have, not only for enjoying your product but also enjoying your shopping experience? For example, a topic in golf retailing right now is whether 18 holes divided into two halves of 9 is the right number, or whether it makes sense to have 3 portions of 6 holes so that people with less time can get in a quick game.

The buyer who buys a sport drink to quench a need for energy is motivated by that need. Motivational data, then, is knowledge that identifies what drives a buyer to make a purchase. To understand wallet size, you have to understand how the buyer sees a purchase, and the buyer sees a purchase based on motivation.

Motivational knowledge is important for both B2C and B2B. In the research I've conducted over the past two decades on how organizations make buying decisions, I've learned that buyers have personal needs as well as organizational needs, and sometimes these personal needs are dominant. To an organizational buyer, the situation may be about showing off decision-making skills or meeting a profit target by cutting expenses, not about choosing benefits from two wonderful products. To be sure, budgets are on paper and more formal. At the same time, there is discretion within those budgets and it helps to understand the motivation underlying customers' choices.

One challenge is determining the size of the wallet; the other is determining life. Back to the young women who shop at the fashion retailer. There is one event that changes forever how they shop—college graduation. Identify that, and you've identified a major change in their shopping habits. Yes, they still buy jeans, but not as many, and not always at the same price since they are now on their own. Nor is the rest of their fashion shopping the same. These shopping changes are driven by their lifestyle changes.

The Opposite Problem

A data trap requires a lot of data to exist. But what if your challenge is just the opposite—a lack of data? Perhaps your organization has a small customer list or perhaps no one kept the data. Does that mean that this DCS approach won't work for you? What do you do?

First, don't put the book down or give it away just yet! The principles of a sound data strategy still apply. In some respects, the data strategy is a bit easier when your universe of customers is smaller. How you go about getting data and storing it will be different as a function of scale, or size. The principles, however, still apply.

Where's the Data?

Part of the allure of transactional data is that it is already there in the enterprise. Motivational and lifestyle data are not; you have to go get them. And that means research (or paying someone for it).

There are two ways to get data: ask or observe. For example, motivational data can be gathered using a sample of several hundred customers. Using Overstock.com again as an example, you can start with focus groups, asking 10 buyers at a time, "What is the biggest benefit you get when you shop at Overstock.com?" If some say, "It's fun," then you know that there is the possibility that there is a fun-seeking group of buyers. Follow this up with a survey of several hundred more customers.

Ask additional questions so that you can understand what they mean by "fun." (Note: focus groups are particularly useful if your population of customers is small.) Alternatively, you could analyze the text of tweets, blogs, and posts and recognize a fun segment is out there.

Similarly, if you have sales people and other front-line customer employees, they probably already have a pretty good idea of what the categories of buyers are. Don't have a lot of money or time to pursue a big marketing research project? Start with the sales force. Simply by asking salespeople what they think, you can identify groups of buyers to start your marketing strategies.

How valuable are these buyers? Hard to say at this point, but that is something you can easily determine with transactional and behavioral data. As suggested earlier, on the 34th day after someone has made a new purchase and using the additional information about what constitutes a "fun" shopping experience on the website, you create and make an offer that should appeal to the fun shopper. You don't have to ask that shopper if he or she is fun-driven—the shopper will tell you by responding either with a purchase or a "delete message." Now you've gathered data and probably made a profit at the same time.

A similar way to ask and receive is through progressive profiling. Progressive profiling is the process of asking questions to learn more about your customer but asking these questions over time. For example, a customer signs up for a newsletter—ask for interests. Then the customer calls the call center to order a product—ask for household composition ("Oh, do you have children? That's a wonderful product for your family to enjoy…"). Hold an event to introduce a new product line—ask for usage information ("How often do you use our product when entertaining?").

As for determining the relative value of the fun shopper versus the hard-core discounter, time will tell you who is more valuable. As you build data on these two groups through both observed behavior and progressive profiling, you'll be able to determine the defined value of each as it stands—*given how you currently market*.

You have an impact on that value. When discounts are offered willy-nilly, the value of the customer base is lower. When offers are appropriately targeted, value curves shift, meaning that some customers increase in value because they respond, whereas others may decline in relative value because they respond to lower-value offers.

Further, acquisition strategies may then change. As relative value of each group becomes known, motivational profiles should be continuously tested. In other words, the motivational (and lifestyle) profile of the group is continuously fleshed out by testing offers and responses, which can then be used to more effectively acquire similar customers.

Case Study: *Gallery Furniture*

If you live in Houston, you know Mattress Mack and that he will "absolutely save you money!" He's justifiably a legend in Houston, not just because of his crazy commercials over the past 30 years but also because he's civic-minded and believes in sharing the wealth of his success.

Mack (nee' James MacEngvale) realized, though, that furniture retailing is changing, just like all consumer purchasing. **Showrooming,** or the practice by consumers of going to a retailer to touch and feel a product before ordering it cheaper online, was beginning to start to become a problem even in furniture. Mack fought it with "Get it TODAY!" delivery, with aggressive pricing, and with clever inventory management and sourcing that makes showrooming next to impossible. If Mack is the only one with a particular product or color, showrooming won't work so he also began to strengthen his custom product line.

What happened wasn't that Mack just defended his market share. He actually grew his sales and his profits.

Even so, Mack wasn't content. He challenged long-held assumptions in retailing, one of which was that customers who leave won't come back to buy. With a strong follow-up program, he's learned just how wrong that assumption is. I can't share all of the details on that program, but what he will let me tell you is this:

- A furniture customer today is likely to change over one full room, and possibly more, in the next 18 months—even if all that was purchased was a wing chair or a mattress.
- Some types of buyers will change over their public areas every three years.

- Find those buyers, capture their hearts, and you have first shot at all of their business.

Now you can draw those first two conclusions from transactional data but if you stop there, you'll fall into a data trap. You've got to add other data, as well as draw and test inferences, to win their affection.

Starting simple, Mack began with a newsletter. The newsletter contained stories that appealed to certain segments. By simply tracking who read what, a clearer picture of who the reader is and what that person is interested in began to appear.

Further, depending on the segment, there are certain events each year that can trigger purchases. Back to school might mean Junior needs a desk, but it might also mean Dad wants a big screen for football (and if he's a Houston Texans fan, custom leather furniture with the Texans logo—can't get that anywhere but through Mack). Yes, you could advertise in the Houston Chronicle, but how much more powerful is it to send those offers directly to the households that might be interested? And, make them a low-cost high value offer (like meet Arian Foster, star running back of the Texans, who is at Gallery Furniture every Tuesday for a radio show during the season) that they can't get anywhere else.

Sounds like just good retailing. But there's a data strategy behind it that includes continuous improvement because success can be tracked back to the offer. That's one problem with advertising—as one famous advertiser said, "I'm sure half of my advertising works. I just don't know which half." With this approach of marketing directly, using data, new data are captured and better offers crafted and presented.

The Rest of a Data Strategy

Data are the foundation of a Dynamic Customer Strategy. Good data is required to understand how variables relate in driving customer behavior, and getting good data means having a sound data strategy. Acquisition of data can include using transactional datasets from your financial data, but it can also include "asking" customers by giving them an offer and seeing if they respond or by asking questions over time.

Summary

Creating a data strategy involves more than simply identifying what data you want or cataloging the data you have. Many decision makers fall prey to data traps but with Big Data, the most common is thinking that a lot of data equates to knowledge. A good data strategy includes acquiring the right data for the decisions to be made, analyzing appropriately, applying the knowledge operationally, and assessing the data and the process for value.

Discussion Questions

1. How can Big Data increase the likelihood of being trapped by data? What's the solution?
2. Are you guilty of showrooming? If so, describe the situation. How close does the in-store price have to be to the online price to get you to buy right then and there? What long term effects do you think showrooming will have on how products are bought?
3. Explain how the quote at the start of the chapter relates to the chapter's topics, as well as how it relates in general to DCS.

CHAPTER 4

Operationalizing Strategy

Who asks whether the enemy was defeated by strategy or valor?
—Virgil

Introduction

How does theory become a strategy? We explore the links between mapping the factors that influence a market and creating action plans to leverage those relationships. After reading this chapter, you should be able to:

- Create operational definitions of the concepts you've identified in a theory
- Develop measures based on those operational definitions
- Design decision rules that trigger marketing actions
- Begin to assess the effectiveness of your measures

By now, you already understand, at least conceptually, that Big Data by itself isn't strategic. In fact, creating rule engines around data such as *Call customer after three visits to the website* isn't strategy either. Such engines support systems, a key part of making strategy work[1]—it's just not strategy.

But what do you do when you've gained new insight into your market through conceptual mapping and realized that you have data to be leveraged for greater value? Here is the chapter when we take the conceptual and make it real, when we go from conceptual to operational.

Conceptual to Operational Definition

If you recall in Chapter 2, we discussed models of loyalty to understand how you build your concept map. One possible model might look like the one in Figure 4.1.

Figure 4.1. A simple model of loyalty.

Conceptually, you may think of customer satisfaction as "the degree to which expectations are met." This definition is one of a handful of commonly-used definitions. For loyalty, how about "the degree to which a customer prefers to use a particular product," or "the proportion of purchases made of the same product." These two definitions of loyalty are conceptually miles apart. One considers how the buyer feels about the product whereas the other simply considers purchasing behavior. As we discussed in Chapter 2, the first reflects attitudinal loyalty whereas the second is behavioral loyalty. Making the distinction is important because you'll do different things to achieve one versus the other.

For example, you may consider attitudinal loyalty more important because having people like your brand is necessary to get positive word of mouth—most students certainly think attitudinal is most important. But without purchasing, attitudinal loyalty may not be worth much. And in some market segments, behavioral may be all you can get. One participant in our study on data cultures identified a particular segment where speed of service was most important.[2] There was no "liking" of any brand,—it was all about speed. Get speed to serve right and you had their business—it was pure behavioral loyalty of the best kind.

Distinguishing between behavioral and attitudinal loyalty, though, doesn't mark the end of the definitional challenge. What did speed to service mean? Did it mean how long they had to wait to get served, how long it took to be served once they talked to a clerk, or how long it took from the point they drove into the parking lot to the point when they left? Or did they really know how to measure it and was their perception something you could influence?

The distinction between these measures isn't unimportant. You've got an entire market segment that wants speed—but if you want to give them what they want, you've got to understand what they mean when they say "fast."

If you want to change loyalty, you have to be able to measure it so you can tell if it changed. In this instance, simply observing frequency of purchase would be one way to measure change. Further, your measure has to reflect your conceptual definition. If you want to influence attitudinal loyalty, your measure isn't going to be frequency of purchase. Yes, you want more sales but that should be an outcome of attitudinal loyalty. Rather your measure may be something like how likely they are to refer you to someone or how they answer a set of questions around their preference for your brand. But is preference the same as loyalty?

To make matters more difficult, your salespeople will talk about customers who are loyal because they always buy something, but at the same time these same customers are buying twice as much from a competitor! Or, marketing thinks these customers love us because they're Platinum cardholders, without realizing that these same buyers are Platinum for three other vendors.

Getting the definition right matters because the definition alters the rules by which your marketing automation engines and sales strategies work. Getting the definition right matters because people in your organization are making decisions based on that definition. When you've got Big Data flying at you at increasing rates, you have to have good operational definitions because these reduce the data into manageable form.

Operational Definition

Yes, you have a conceptual definition but to work with Big Data, you also need operational definitions. You might know that your marketing is supposed to create a qualified lead and conceptually, you know that a lead is someone ready to receive a sales call, but specifically, what makes a lead *qualified*? How will you put that into practice?

An **operational definition** is how you measure the concept, and, in this instance, set a standard to determine the label. We all operationalize concepts like quality in our everyday life. Quality is a conceptual term. For example, think about how you try to figure out which product has higher quality when you're shopping and you don't have any experience with that product to guide your evaluation. When you look at a product that costs $10 and another that costs $15, you assume the higher priced product is of higher quality if you have no other basis for that judgment.

As marketers, we also have to turn concepts like perceived quality into concrete measures, actions, and standards. For example, let's go back to our need to create a qualified lead.

Conceptually, a qualified lead is someone who is ready to receive a sales call; that is, relative to others drawn from the same pool, this person or this business is more likely to buy. That pool could be a list from the phone book, attendees at a trade show, or licensed dog owners, depending on what you are selling. Once the individual has shown some level of interest, you engage in certain marketing activities to get that individual to the point where she or he is ready to engage with a salesperson. What makes a lead a qualified lead will depend on what sales wants or what has been shown to lead to sales but you'll need that definition.

Some examples of operational definitions of qualified leads:

1. Business has X number of employees
2. Browsed the website X number of times
3. Downloaded a white paper
4. Visited the trade show booth and rated a qualified lead by the booth staff

As you can see, none of these are very far down the path of purchasing, but then again, they're just leads. Which one is the best definition? Clearly, the first one is pretty weak. We have no indication of interest at all. Perhaps the last has shown the greatest level of interest, but the real answer has to come from your sales staff. If you are trying to generate qualified leads, what separates qualified from unqualified is whether they are ready to receive a sales call, and that varies from market to market.

Further, get it wrong and it won't take long before salespeople quit trusting any leads. If you give them a list based only on the number of website visits, for example, it won't take a day before they realize these are people who, for the most part, are not ready to receive a sales call.

So what is the behavior or marker that indicates that they are ready? Once you find that out, you have an operational definition of a qualified lead and you can begin to direct marketing activities to move unqualified leads to qualified leads.

The operational definition also describes how the concept will be measured. If a qualified lead is to meet a specified level of certain characteristics, then those characteristics define the measure.

Since few companies engage in only one marketing activity (e.g. trade shows), **lead scoring models** are developed that weigh the relative readiness of a potentially qualified lead to receive a sales call. Look back at the list. We could assign a point value to each item: say 2 points for #1 and 5 points for #4. When the total value of points reaches 10, we then have a qualified lead. Some lead scoring models are far more sophisticated but most are not.

Some well-known variables that are really operational definitions of concepts include:

- Net promoter score[3] as a way to operationalize customer satisfaction.
- Loyalty program level (e.g., Silver, Gold, Platinum) as a way to operationalize customer value
- Gartner's Magic Quadrant® score of technology providers and *US News & World Report* rankings of universities as ways to operationalize overall quality, at least as they define quality.

One way to tame Big Data, then, is through good operational definitions. Good operational definitions serve the purpose of reducing data down to important judgments. You may have all types of data as part of your lead scoring model for determining lead qualification but once you create the definition, all of those observations and variables become one variable with only two values: lead or not a lead. And that's far more manageable.

From Strategy to Action

Of course, strategy isn't about defining some nebulous concept but rather about doing things that accomplish objectives. Strategy is about making choices, selecting from alternatives the route you'll take. But which alternatives,—what actions? If you want to create loyalty, what actions should you take? This set of decisions is where your conception of how which factors influence the outcomes you are hoping for becomes so important.

For example, if you want to create habits (behavioral loyalty), such as Target was trying to do through its promotions aimed at expectant mothers, the habits are the objectives and we know from research how many times actions have to be taken over a period of time to become a habit. That understanding then informs our action plans, if we're Target, regarding how often we present an offer to that expectant mother.

Since strategy is about making choices, let's take a look at decision making in organizations. In particular, we'll start with some of the barriers that can make effective decision making less likely.

Barriers to Effective Use of Big Data

Many current management practices and, in some instances, the ethos of today's management culture actually make effective decision making with Big Data more difficult. The problem isn't that decisions are left unmade; it's just that the best decision may get missed.

A Bias for Action

The quote at the start of this chapter may be old,—even ancient —but it still reflects the bias for action that can stymie real progress. To be a leader of action is highly desirable, it seems. Too often, though, a bias for action is simply a euphemism for too-lazy-to-do the necessary-due-diligence and fail fast an excuse for mistakes.

Yet, one of the characteristics of Big Data is velocity. The velocity at which data comes at us is increasing, as is the rate at which we have to make decisions. Thus, the greater velocity of data creates yet another trap by making a bias for action seem even more important than ever.

How does a bias for action hurt decision making? One way is a failure to consider all of the alternatives. In decision making research, they call this commitment—the tendency to commit to a course of action too early.

An alternative, though, is to set up data systems so that waiting for data isn't long or expensive. The velocity of Big Data can, with the right decision support system, improve decision making speed. I'm not advocating that waiting for all of the data is always better; rather, I'm saying that Big Data has the power to improve the chances of a bias for action succeeding, if the right systems are in place. We'll talk more about some of those systems when we talk about application in Chapters 5 and 6. For now, although you may not have time to stop and smell the roses, at least stop and force yourself to brainstorm a list of alternatives before you select a course of action. Otherwise, you are likely to settle on a course of action and then use the data to support the decision you made, rather than using the data to make a decision.

Further, research shows that if you can sleep on a decision just one night, the chances are much higher that you'll make a better decision.[4] Just one night! So if you have a big decision to make, sleep on it.

Numbers Myopia

A second way that decision making is hurt is in how the numbers get interpreted or presented. The classic research in this area asked people questions such as, "If you had a treatment for an epidemic but half the people you used it on would die, would you use it?" Most would say no. "If you had a treatment for an epidemic that saved the lives of half of the people you used it on, would you use it?" Most would say yes. In both cases, half die, half live; the only difference was whether the choice was framed as a gain or as a loss.

Similarly, I teach a case where the reader is told that 30% of first-time visitors to a horseracing track don't come back. Students (whether execs or undergrads) always assume that to be a bad situation, but flip it. If you could count on 70% of your first-timers to come back, you would be pretty happy. Further, looking at the two alternatives—that is, either first-timers are not coming back or first-timers are coming back—the follow up questions change completely and the alternatives for action are very different.

We are primed, as human beings, to avoid loss.[5] Study after study shows how we try to avoid loss, pain, or suffering, and that we prefer avoiding pain to realizing gain. That fact of human nature has wide reaching consequences. But how numbers are presented to us can cause us to focus on the negative, allowing our natural tendency to avoid loss to overwhelm our decision making, causing us to lose sight of what we can gain.

So think for a minute about what can happen when a bias for action combines with numbers myopia. What happens when you are prone to acting quickly but misread the truth that is behind the numbers? Discounts get offered too quickly, product lines get cancelled, and other ways to miss opportunities are realized. Before you act, make it a common practice to flip numbers (to turn that 30% leaving rate into a 70% staying rate), then see if you still find a course of action desirable. And again, sleep on it!

Data Trust

Another limiting factor is a lack of trust in data. This lack of trust takes two forms: the hero ethos and the *not-invented-here (NIH)* syndrome.

The hero ethos is a trap leaders can fall into when they take themselves a bit too seriously and believe they can, or need to, do it all. They trust their gut because their gut hasn't let them down and even if it has, they blame that failure on some other factor. After all, they are the Chief Executive Officer (CEO), or the Chief Marketing Officer (CMO)! Actual CEOs and CMOs are less likely to fall into this trap than are CEO-wannabes but even so, their bias for action coupled with their ego makes it difficult for someone with numbers to rely on the numbers to sell an idea.

NIH is just the not-invented-here syndrome applied to data. If it's not my data, I can't trust it. The decision maker with NIH can't trust anyone else's data. Without confidence in how the data were gathered, what exactly was the question asked, how were the data analyzed, and so forth, this data scientist remains skeptical and frozen to action.

In a study published by Pitney Bowes, some 9% of data scientists said their biggest challenge in unlocking the value of Big Data is that their upper management team doesn't see the value in Big Data.[6] Perhaps one of the most famous data skeptics is the CEO of Starbucks. "Howard [Schultz] doesn't care about data. He has absolutely no head for data," said Joe LaCugna, director of analytics and business intelligence at Starbucks during a session at the Big Data Retail Forum in Chicago.[7] (I wonder if LaCugna got called in to explain that remark.) But add to the 9% of upper management who fail to trust data another 11% with a culture of not trusting data, and you can see the opportunity is there to beat out at least one-fifth of your competitors by simply using data effectively.

A Case Study: Random House

A very simple example of Dynamic Customer Strategy (DCS) involves the book, *Defending Jacob*, published by Random House.[8] This suspense novel by William Landay tells the story of a district attorney defending his son in a murder case. When Random House launched the book, they ran a limited ad campaign designed to reach a certain demographic, mostly men because men are the typical thriller audience. As they listened to readers' comments in social media and online focus groups, however, they realized that the book resonated strongly with a different group, and for a different reason, than they had planned. Moms and other readers focused more on the parenting relationships in the story, a very different audience than the masculine one that reaches for traditional thrillers. Random House then changed their ad copy and placement strategy to reach more moms.

At its simplest, this example could be viewed as just a miscalculation on the part of the publisher. Conceptually, they know that thrillers are read by more men; parenting stories by more women and those two relationships did not change. But that's the point—DCS doesn't necessarily mean that you change your conceptual map of how your market works. Yes, DCS can mean that you learn that your conceptual map is wrong but more often than not, the challenge lies in operationalizing well; in this case, recognizing what kind of story they had to work with, then using their pre-existing conceptual map to re-target their approach.

The second important aspect of this case study is how they implemented a fail fast, fail cheap approach to learning. Applying a limited marketing budget coupled with online focus groups enabled them to get the book out and see how the book fared before making a full investment. We hear about *Defending Jacob* because the alteration in strategy was ultimately successful; we don't hear about the books that completely failed because many don't get a full launch if they can't make it out of the test market.

Creating Decision Rules

After creating operational definitions of the concepts and determining what actions you want to take to reach your objectives, the next step is putting it into action.

One aspect of Big Data that many are overlooking, however, is that Big Data gives us the ability to implement the type of personalized marketing that CRM has been promising for almost two decades. Essentially, what gets created is a network of If/Then rules, decision rules that allow your marketing technology or sales/service staff to determine what action to take when.

If my lead score is a 5, then have a call center agent call; if below 5, then send the next email in the campaign. If the lead downloads a white paper, send Email #3 two days later. These are simple decision rules but remember that a lead score can actually be a composite measure of whether the lead browsed the website, visited the booth at a trade show, or any combination of activities. The decision rule may appear simple but the operational definitions behind it may be complex.

Decision rules can play another role, too. When experimenting, hypotheses actually should be thought of as decision rules.

Typically, in an A/B test (where A is tested against B), the hypothesis is something like this: I think A might work better than B. So one is run against the other and whichever performs better is the one used.

Simple hypotheses like that get much more difficult to test, though, when you are testing several at a time. Using advanced forms of experimental design, you can literally test A through Z simultaneously. As you can imagine, determining whether F is better than S can be pretty tricky with so many.

Further, if you remember Type I and Type II error from your statistics class, you know that Type I is the error made when you decide that there's a difference but there really isn't, and Type II is when you fail to recognize a difference when one exists. Like most students, you probably just thought of these errors as statistical things to be forgotten after the tests.

The reality is that these are forms of decision risk that you can influence. Think about it from this standpoint: a decision maker makes a Type I error when he decides to invest in the new marketing strategy when in fact the old marketing strategy was just as good. Type I error is equivalent, in that example, to investment risk because the decision maker is making an investment without gain.

Alternatively, Type II error is the same as opportunity risk. In this instance, Plan B is better, but the decision maker fails to recognize it and fails to capitalize on the opportunity.

If you recall from your stats class, we usually decide that there's a difference between A and B if p is less than .05. That decision rule assumes that investment risk is more important. Your statistician can actually alter decision rules to control the amount of statistical risk you are taking in both investment and opportunity risk. The thing for you to remember is that by reducing p, you are reducing investment risk but you are not directly affecting opportunity risk. That's actually a different statistic and your statistician can help you with that so talk over Type I and Type II error if you are dealing with a really big decision.

Summary

Operational definitions take the concepts and make them real. An operational definition can be a standard (such as a lead is someone who scores above X on a series of measures) or a measure (the degree of loyalty is their Recency, Frequency, and Monetary score). Once we operationalize the concepts, we can begin to create the actions that will influence those factors that will move customers and markets toward our objectives. But a bias for action and numbers myopia can inhibit our ability to use Big Data. To use data more effectively, we can create decision rules that consider both investment risk and opportunity risk.

Discussion Questions

1. Explain the difference between an operational definition and a conceptual definition as if you were talking with an executive. Give an example of an operational definition and the concept it represents from your favorite television commercial or brand.
2. How do you know how much to favor action over careful thinking and planning? In other words, how do you know the optimal balance

between acting quickly or thinking through? What are the implications for the DCS strategist? List three characteristics of a decision that might lead you to either act quicker or invest more in gathering information.

3. Of the barriers to effectively using Big Data listed in the chapter, which do you think is the most difficult for a company or manager to overcome, and why?

CHAPTER 5

Acquiring Big (and Little) Data

If we have data, let's look at data. If all we have are opinions, let's go with mine.

—Jim Barksdale, former Netscape CEO

Introduction

Big (and little) data are as necessary to Dynamic Customer Strategy (DCS) as food is to a teenager. With a voracious appetite, DCS seeks data that can provide any additional edge. In this chapter, we dive deeper into the acquisition stage of data strategy. At the end, you'll be able to:

- Identify new sources of data that add quality to decisioning
- Assess the quality of measures, given your conceptual map
- Create a plan for sourcing data

Do we have the data? If not, the best we can do is offer an opinion. And if you follow the quote to the ultimate conclusion regarding Netscape's outcomes, perhaps Barksdale's opinion was not enough.

Too much data of the same type, though, results in data traps; that is, getting lots of data but really it's just a lot of data points for the same variable. And if you recall, we then infer that someone really appreciates the clean clothes that come out of our washing machines only to find that they're really making cheese.

The cheese problem is created when trying to make decisions with the data we can get cheaply and easily, rather than the data we really need to solve the problem or make the decision. Data traps can lead to other inferential errors and companies can create a cheese problem even without a data trap. For example, marketers used to make decisions about broadcast advertising effectiveness based on Nielsen ratings because Nielsen data were all that were available; now they can also include social media measures of engagement thanks to Bluefin Labs or Nielsen's joint venture with Twitter. But the real question is whether these are the right measures for *your* business, rather than only easy measures to buy.

With Big Data, the challenge isn't always about choosing the right data from a myriad choice sets; rather, the challenge can be how to get the right data. But before we can figure out where the data reside, we need to understand what data we need. And sometimes, that means going outside traditional data fields for new ways to look at old questions.

So what data do we need? Where is it? What will it cost to acquire? Where do we start?

The right place to start is with the question we're trying to answer. If you were Cabela's and trying to answer the question: "What events create sales opportunities?" Take a moment and reflect on what that list of events might include.

Probably first to your mind were things like birthdays, gift-giving holidays, and the like. Then, you may have thought about events like moving, which might necessitate new clothing. Or you may have thought about the weather, and the effects different types of weather might have on a particular outdoor trip (turns out that's not a good predictor of a sales opportunity but we'll get into that later). Or you may have considered events such as buying a hunting or fishing license for the first time.

Recall the Target case study. In that case study, the event was a woman's pregnancy.

Now think about the data needed to find these events. What data do we need? Where is it? What will it cost to acquire? In Target's case, they had the data already; they just needed to organize it in a meaningful way. For Cabela's, they may not. If the event is moving, then hunting and fishing license data purchased from state fish and game departments may provide the key.

One tool that can help is a Data Assets Inventory. A **data assets inventory** is a matrix, not a list, of what data you do have by variable and source. You can think of it as a spreadsheet comprised of all of the headers of all of your data files but organized by variable category. All household data, for example, would be listed in the same columns. If you had customer address as a variable and you had this variable in twelve different files, you'd have one column for address but the variable would appear twelve times.

Consider segmentation. You've got RFM scores (recency of purchase, frequency of purchase within a specified time, and monetary value or average purchase value) to determine the relative value of a customer to you. And, you've got that by product category so you can tell if someone likes to hike or hunt, or hike and hunt. Now, just on the basis of transaction data, you've got maybe 15 segments (5 levels of customer value by 3 product category combinations). But there's a lot more to segmentation and your data assets inventory can help you identify other variables that might help in segmenting more finely. For example, you may find that your hunter has a license to hunt in another state—hmmm, that means this hunter travels and spends a lot on hunting. But without looking at the data assets inventory and recognizing that "state of license" is a variable, you may have missed it.

Before we dive into the various sources of data, there are some characteristics about data quality that we need to understand first. Although this subject can sometimes seem tedious—some of this is quite academic in nature—the consequences of understanding are too important to not pay attention.

Measurement Quality

You could ask your customer, "How loyal are you?" and they might reply, "Very." But what does that really mean? Does it mean that you have someone who will recommend you to friends? Someone who will put up with an occasional bad experience? Or someone who feels warm inside when they see your logo or hear your jingle?

You could track their purchases. When given a choice, do they still pick you? What do you call it when they don't have a choice? Try buying a Coke at DFW Airport—you can't. They only sell Pepsi products. If I drink tea instead of the offered Pepsi, am I being disloyal to Coke? If you're tracking my purchases, how can you tell?

Clearly, you want accurate measures. **Accuracy** is the degree to which measure reflects reality. But in the context of DCS, one dimension of accuracy is also the degree to which the measure reflects the concept and the reality of the concept. As a simple example, if we want behavioral loyalty, we need a behavioral measure. But having a behavioral measure is not enough; in our Coke example, we have to be able to account for situations like DFW Airport if our measure is to reflect our concept.

The second characteristic is precision. **Precision**, also known as reliability, is the ability of a measurement system or device to produce the same result over time when faced with the same conditions. For example, Arbitron, a marketing research firm, asks listeners to fill out a diary of what they listen to on the radio, but what Pandora listeners hear can be tracked automatically–tracking has added precision. Precision is lost by Arbitron because the diary measure relies on people filling out a diary while they still recall what they listened to, for how long, and at what time. Yet, there may be value in the Arbitron measure because it is a measure of what people remember, so it may add information about the strength of listening. Further, Pandora may precisely record what is played but fail to capture what was listened to—the user may have stepped away and left it playing. This example illustrates the importance of knowing how a measure was created.

Another example may help with the concepts of precision and accuracy. When you visit another country and someone asks where you are from, you may say America. Or you may say Texas. Perhaps even Waco. But if you gave latitude and longitude (31.5° north, 14.46° west), then your answer is incredibly accurate—not precise. What is precise is the GPS tool or Google map you used to determine your answer.

Precision and Big Data

Some argue that precision is one form or cause of big data. The argument is that our measures are more precise, and that adds data points. Just as important, precision gives us data that is useful in more ways. In both cases, you still only have one measure so how is precision related to big data? This question really centers attention on the concept of **triangulation**. If I have only Pandora listenership, then I miss out on the XM-Sirius activity in your car, for example, and that takes more data

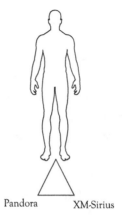

Pandora   XM-Sirius

Figure 5.1. By gathering listening data from at least 2 sources (Pandora and XM-Sirius), we can fix on the listener's habits more accurately through triangulation.

points and more data makes for big data (Figure 5.1). Thus, precision doesn't really mean big data; rather, the ability to take more measurements precisely adds to big data. And yes, we'd have to also have other possible sources of music in our data collection process.

If you are Cabela's and I am your customer, I may buy online, in the store, or via the telephone while using a printed catalog. If I buy online, you know it is me and not my wife because I log in on my account. If I use my Discover card and not my Cabela's card while I'm in the store, you may know it came from my household but you don't know whether it was me. The online transaction is more precise than the in-store, in this instance, because you not only know the household, you know the individual.

Yet, knowing that it was me may not give you a very clear picture of who I am. Yes, you have a name and an address, but can you put me into a market segment with any degree of confidence? No, your data lacks that type of precision. **Inferential precision** is the degree to which you can draw a conclusion (an inference) based on the data. And better inferential precision also leads to big data value—the more data points we have, the more precise we can be when drawing conclusions or making inferences by applying triangulation.

Back again to the loyalty example. If you want to know if I am a loyal Cabela's shopper, then you want to make an inference, the inference being "he's a loyal (or not) shopper." If I buy something once a month, am I loyal? That depends—what else do I buy in the category and from whom?

Any grocer worth his salt knows, given the size of your household and your average purchase quantity, how often you need to buy toilet paper. Yes, it would creep me out if I got something from my grocer saying it's time to fill the bathroom cabinet, but at the same time, the grocer can look at my average purchase history and identify whether I'm loyal in my TP purchases, and then take action to alter my behavior if need be. With subtlety, just as Target learned in presenting offers related to pregnancy, that grocer can make me an offer on toilet paper that won't creep me out and perhaps lead to additional revenue.

Having the right data needed to make good marketing decisions is the goal with measurement and why accuracy is important. If the measure is inaccurate, imprecise, and inferentially poor, then someone will spend money on bad marketing.

Sources and Big Data

With today's information technology, organizations can combine apparently disparate sources of information to dig deeper and yield new insights. Some of the more interesting applications of Big Data occur when these data are combined and analyzed.

Variety

One of the three Vs of Big Data is *Variety*. Variety in data is important because that's what gives us the ability to triangulate on the truth. When data scientists were talking about trying to get to a 360° view of the customer, they were really describing triangulating on who that customer is. That requires a variety of data—just the opposite of a data trap.

Big Data technology now makes orthogonal data sources useful. The term comes from math, where orthogonal means two dimensions that are completely independent, and can therefore be arrayed as perpendicular (at 90° angles). When we use the term **orthogonal data** in the context of Big Data, we mean data from independent sources that are seemingly unconnected.

Let's say, for example, that you want to find lead users. A **lead user**[1] is a customer who is so innovative with how your product is used that you can actually commercialize her or his ideas into new products or new markets. For example, the cheese makers were lead users; the appliance manufacturer actually developed a cheese-making machine based on their original and innovative use of the product.

One way you would find lead users is by looking at speaker lists at conferences—people who are innovative are asked to speak about it. That source of information would be independent of your customer list, but you may cross-reference the two lists and then send an engineer to those customers on both lists to see what they're doing.

What if you were able to corroborate expertise in a certain area (say, something like Hadoop® or some other technology) with innovation? What data sources could help you there? How about LinkedIn® profiles? Or resumes of job seekers and the companies they worked for? Both LinkedIn® profiles and online resume databases have actually been used to identify leads for certain types of products based on the assumption that a large group of people with a certain skill set predicts a certain set of activity (in fact, the CIA has used resume-scraping as a way to identify possible sites of certain activities that I'm not allowed to write about).

What if, though, our lead users are consumers, not professionals? How could we identify expert consumer users? Sometimes, it's easiest to simply ask, so don't get too carried away trying to find alternative sources of data. The point is that sometimes, seemingly unrelated data can signal important characteristics about your market.

Does magazine subscription cancellation or non-renewal signal a decrease in household earnings or a change in household make-up? Might that signal an opportunity—especially if we could also match that up to changes in household consumption based on our own transactional data? Can subscription data also help identify movers?

Of course, I'm merely speculating—putting seemingly disparate data together to identify something about my customer. That's the point, however. With today's data technology, we can begin to link disparate data sources to the data we have and draw new inferences.

An important rule of thumb, though, is to remember that it takes about twice as much time to prepare data for analysis as it does to actually analyze it. Further, the more disparate the data, the more likely it will take some time to bring structure to it. For example, the first step in analyzing text data is to convert the text into numbers, a process that can be automated but even so, it requires thought and time.

Progressive Profiling

Simple is best. One of the simplest ways to get customer data is to ask. Oftentimes, though, we think we have to pay for the response so we offer discounts in exchange for asking. Let's examine what JC Penney learned about how to ask for customer data.

Case Study: JC Penney

JC Penney, before the big debacle over the switch to an everyday low pricing strategy, wanted to launch the Ambrielle line of lingerie. Ambrielle was launched to replace their previous private label brand, which was simply known as JC Penney Intimates, and had been experiencing declining sales.

The new brand, though, had to represent an improvement in actual product quality. Intimates was doing poorly as a brand because product quality had fallen behind Victoria's Secrets in particular, and all of the other brands in general, that were capturing market share. While the exercise of product design for quality is a traditional marketing research challenge, Laura Carros and others at JCP Penney saw this situation for the opportunity it was—to not only learn what consumers wanted, but to also develop relationships with women who could help maintain that product design edge.

To start, JCP had to identify women who were lead users, and in this instance those women who were fashion-aware about lingerie, influenced other women, and were willing to partner with a retailer to participate in the product design process. The decision was made to send out a postcard to 100,000 women, known customers of JCP, and ask them to go online and sign up for the Ambrielle panel. When they signed up, they were asked a series of questions to determine if they qualified as lead users; if they failed to qualify, they were thanked for their time and offered a coupon.

When you send out the postcard, what would it say?

At the last minute, some of the leadership at JCP panicked. "We're not offering them anything to participate! We won't get any response!" So they turned the postcard into a coupon, to be redeemed online after registering on the site.

Then, cooler heads prevailed and said, "Hey, this is a testable hypothesis. Let's randomly split the list into two and offer the incentive to only half and see what pulls better." (That's an advantage of having a history in catalog and direct mail, by the way; there is a long tradition of testing and experimentation that makes these kinds of decisions easier and avoids the kind of thinking exemplified by the Barksdale quote at the start of this chapter.)

By now, it's probably no surprise that the postcard without the incentive outdrew the postcard with the incentive. What may be surprising is that the no-incentive version outdrew the incentive version by almost ten to one. The incentive drew at a normal dismal rate of about 2%. Yes, the non-incentive was almost 20%.

Although many of those women did not qualify as lead users, several important lessons were learned. First, consumers who see themselves as lead users want to participate in what they view as a legitimate opportunity. The incentive signaled that this offer was not a legitimate opportunity to participate in a co-creation process. Rather, the incentive signaled that JCP was interested only in making a sale.

Second, the data they received through the qualification process had value beyond the selection of a panel. Not only could JCP learn valuable insights about the women who participated, they could then start to use that data to create an ongoing conversation with them, whether or not they were invited on to the panel. Further, those women who were not invited to the panel had already signaled a willingness to share data.

This realization led to a different data collection strategy. Whereas the lead user panel actively engaged in activities such as online focus groups, style shows, surveys, and the like, the other women also formed a panel of sorts. Even though they may not have been fashion forward, influential, or one of the other characteristics required to be a lead user, they still had value to offer.

To claim this value, JCP began a process of progressive profiling. **Progressive profiling** is the process of collecting data through various means about specific customers to understand their motivations, consumption patterns, and other characteristics. If you think of online behavior as a form of communication, then you can see how someone at JCP observing a consumer's behavior online or in a store might be prodded to ask questions about motivation, usage situations, and so forth. Progressive profiling is the result. The combination of both brief surveys (two or three questions at a time) and web-browsing data provides deep insight into consumption patterns.

Do we need or want to progressively profile all of our customers? Yes, to some degree we do. But that doesn't mean we need to engage all of our customers into active profiling. **Active profiling** involves direct questioning and observation; in most instances, companies should engage in active profiling with a sample of customers just to manage costs.

Inferential profiling can then be accomplished with the rest of the customer base. **Inferential profiling** is the process of developing customer insight through customer reactions to offers and other customer behaviors.

1. We create our profiles through active profiling with a sample
2. We then apply those profiles to our customer population.

If our inferences are correct, customers who were inferentially profiled based on data similar to the active profiles should behave similarly. If they don't, we've learned additional information that we can use for further profiling.

Volume

Another characteristic of Big Data and the technology that allows mastery of Big Data is *Volume*, or simply the amount of data we can store and process. Because of the volume we can store and analyze, progressive profiling is possible.

For successful progressive profiling, think *conversation*. For example, if you were JCP and you have a panel member on your site looking at a particular piece of intimate apparel, you might have a pop-up avatar say,

"Aren't these really cute? Some of our consumers pick these for a special night out while others just like feeling special every day. Which one is most like you?"

Note that this same avatar can also make pairing suggestions and carry the conversation in other ways. Each response by the consumer is another piece of data that then adds to her profile.

Further, sampling techniques can be applied to reduce consumer wear-out. If you had to answer three questions every time you went to a retailer's website, you'd quickly stop shopping there. By applying sampling techniques usually used to for experimental designs, you can accomplish precision in profiling without having to ask everyone the same questions. For example, if you have 90 questions you want to ask and 90 similar people to ask, you could ask 1 question per person and assume that the other 89 would answer in a similar fashion. Of course, it's a silly and extreme example—you'd want to ask more than one person. But if you have 9000 people, you could ask 1 question of 100 each and have the volume of data you'd require. We won't get into detail on partial factorial designs; we'll leave that to the data scientists.

Velocity

Variety in Big Data also represents the growing number of sources of data. To make matters more difficult, the rate of speed, or *Velocity*, with which these data are received is intense.

Most marketers don't know what to do with this data; therefore, they don't do anything with it.

Often, though, that may be exactly the right decision.

When faced with seemingly overwhelming Big Data (Velocity, Variety, & Volume), ask yourself, "What decision am I trying to make?" The decision may be which positioning strategy to use or where to set price, or it may be to place a buyer into a micro-segment. Whatever the decision, whether it be market-level (positioning) or consumer level (placing a buyer into a micro-segment), the decision drives the choice of data. That means that the operational definition has to match the conceptual relationship. If, for example, you want to know whether a new commercial works, you need to have data that matches your concept of what *works* means. If by works, you mean it creates awareness, then measure awareness. But, if you want an increase in sales, measure sales.

The second consideration is whether the sample matches the population. Let's say, for example, that you have a new line of energy drinks and want to know which flavor to retain and which to eliminate. Sentiment analysis using data from posts on Twitter, Facebook, and other places might give you an idea. **Sentiment analysis** is the study of text to understand the general direction of how the writer(s) feels about something; you can use it to determine an individual's feelings or an overall measure of the market. If you are trying to decide which flavor to keep, sentiment analysis of social media may be fine. But if you are trying to predict which candidate will win an upcoming election, you should know that Twitter tends to be dominated by people at extreme ends of the political spectrum, and much more so by people who favor liberal candidates. Thus, the population of Twitter may not match the voting population, so the sample of data collected may not match what you would find if you sampled voters. Whereas sentiment analysis is the right kind of analysis for the decision, the data have to match the decision, which in this case, the population from which you took the data has to match the population about which you are making a decision.

One caveat: all too often, a choice of data is based on what is readily and cheaply available. Choosing sentiment analysis because you can easily buy those results is inviting disaster if the sample doesn't match your population or if what you need to measure is referrals, not sentiment. More data is not more knowledge, nor is all knowledge of equal application value. All data has value, it's just that some data is worth a lot more.

Once You've Got It

Once you've acquired the data, you can't just rush into Chapter 6 and start applying analytical models. Two other steps, at least, are needed. The first is data cleaning and the second, not necessarily in that order, is data definition.

Data cleaning is the process by which you prepare the data for analysis, and can involve many steps depending on the original nature of the data. For example, if you have a set of survey data, you have to determine what someone meant when she checked two boxes on a question that is supposed to have only one answer. You also have to make decisions about how to treat inconsistent responses; for example, how do you treat the customer who says he never bought your product but he uses it twice a week? Or says he's never bought it in time period 2 but said he did in time period 1?

Some estimates are that you spend 70% of your time getting data ready for analysis, compared to only 30% actually analyzing it—at least the first time. With Big Data, that proportion is probably accurate or even low. Combining orthogonal data, using unstructured data—all of it takes time to convert it into usable data.

One step in that process is **data definition**, or applying the conceptual label to the data. For example, you may have multiple customer IDs in your data. In a B2B setting, one might have been created by shipping, another by billing, and another by the credit department. Or in retailing, you may have multiple customer IDs representing different members of the same household. Which one really represents a customer? And what happens if you have different IDs for each of the devices that the same customer uses? Combining these and defining which one really represents the customer is an important step in preparing your data for analysis.

In our study of retailers' data maturity, we spoke with one executive who reported mounting frustration because her discussions with peers were hampered by multiple definitions of the same variables. As a result, each exec had a different view of reality. These conflicting views led to challenges in coming to agreement on strategies. As a consequence, she was pushing for the creation of a data inventory, much as we described, whereby each variable would be named and defined, defined both conceptually and operationally (meaning, where the data is acquired, how it is scaled, etc.).

Summary

With Big Data comes many choices about which data to use. Big Data adds precision, both in terms of measurement and inference. Through multiple data sources, we can triangulate on the truth, increasing our confidence in the inferences we make. Further, we can use orthogonal data to deepen our understanding and create new insights.

Progressive profiling is also possible, thanks to Big Data technology. By maintaining behavioral, transactional, and attitudinal data over time, we can triangulate on our consumer; sampling techniques also increase the precision of progressive profiling and triangulation.

But with so many new data sources, the basic questions of whether the measure reflects the concept and how closely does the sample matches the population are often overlooked. What is cheap and easy is not always best.

Discussion Questions

1. JC Penney has struggled under the current leadership, first changing its strategy from regular sales to everyday low (or at least same) pricing, then going back to offering regular sales. How would you have applied the concepts in this chapter to help them avoid making what is viewed by many as a possibly fatal error? (If you are unfamiliar with their plight, do a little bit of internet browsing to get more details.)

2. Identify a brand that you feel knows who you are very well. What evidence can you point to that illustrates that they know you very well? Contrast that with a company that you feel doesn't know you very well. How would understanding the concept of inferential precision help them? What data should they get to improve inferential precision and how would they get it?

3. "Understanding why a customer says no can be just as important as why she says yes." Why? But a customer who says no isn't likely to tell you. How can you use concepts like progressive profiling to fulfill that quote?

CHAPTER 6

Analytics for the Rest of Us

There are three types of lies: lies, damn lies, and statistics.
—Leonard H. Courtney

Introduction

That quote is often attributed to Mark Twain, but no matter who said it first, there is a simple truth there. How do statistics lie to us? They are just numbers after all—right? Well, there may be a bit more to it. Some of our mis-interpretation is human nature and the way we process numbers (you may recall numbers myopia from Chapter 4); other challenges are simply a function of being overwhelmed by the numbers. In this chapter, the objective is not to try to turn you into a statistician. Remember, you can outsource the stats. Rather, you should be able to:

- Recognize the limitations of statistical models
- Understand the application of different model types
- Evaluate model design given data type

The numbers don't lie—but our ability to interpret those numbers can sure vary. And if we want to compete on analytics, we better have a pretty good understanding of what the analytics can and cannot do.

Remember that strategy is about making decisions, exercising options, and selecting alternatives. With better information comes better decisions. The challenge then becomes selecting the right statistical analysis needed to make the best decision.

Applications of Analytics

There are several ways to think about analytics. The first is what you are probably used to from your statistics classes—pose a hypothesis and apply statistics to see what the truth is. For example, you may have wanted to see if a certain marketing mix increased sales in an experiment across a set of stores, or forecast sales for the next year given a set of leading indicators. This process is the **discovery** process (or can be thought of as the discovery stage), and the types of applications are called **research analytics** or research statistics; that is, the application of statistics to answer research questions. Into this category go test and learn projects but you'll also find the type of historical analysis such as we did with Cabela's to identify basket starters.

The second type we will call reporting analytics. **Reporting analytics** are fairly simple math equations, the outcomes of which tell us something about the state of our business. You encountered such types of analytics in managerial accounting and finance classes when you learned about ratios such as the quick ratio. One frequent use of reporting analytics is to standardize outcomes; for example, P/E ratio (or the stock price divided by earnings) provides a way to compare the relative value of stocks. Similarly, sales per square foot is a measure of how well a store performs given its spatial resources. Your stores may be different shapes and sizes but sales per square foot allows you to compare across stores. You may not have thought of these types of measures as a form of analytics but recognizing that these are an application of math helps make the next step to understanding more advanced use of analytics.

The third is **operational analytics**, also known as **production analytics** or the automated application of analytics to dynamic marketing. **Dynamic marketing** is altering presentation of marketing messages based on individual customer characteristics. For example, you search for flights to Lilongwe, Malawi. KLM flies to Africa and so you search KLM.com for flights. Then you notice that KLM is among the banner ads every time you search on Google for weeks afterward. Why? Dynamic marketing algorithms are recognizing you as someone who might be interested in flying on KLM.

Amazon could be considered the father and mother of operational analytics and dynamic marketing. Their "people who bought this also bought that" recommendations are created through **affinity analysis**, a form of analysis that discovers what things tend to occur together. **Market basket analysis** is the study of "what shoppers buy together" or at the same time, the context in which we use affinity analysis to come up with marketing decisions. (Affinity analysis has its use in non-marketing applications, such as seeing what symptoms tend to occur together to help doctors make better diagnoses.) Urban legend has it that Wal-Mart found that beer and diapers are often purchased together so the company moved the two next to each other and increased sales but there's no evidence to support that story—it seems just as likely that Wal-Mart put the two on opposite ends of the store and sold more of everything in-between.

Amazon's form of dynamic marketing is fairly simple. Ramp that dynamic marketing up a few notches to create a probability score, such as that created by Target when identifying potentially pregnant women. A woman makes a purchase one day, then a few days later she makes another, then another, and later yet one more. Each of those purchases is worth, say, a few points. When the total number of points is greater than 10 (or some other number based on the analytics), she is scored as a potentially pregnant woman and a promotional mailer is sent to her home.

Let's look at another example. You are a frequent flyer on United and you ask for an upgrade. United uses a point system based on analysis of customer flight history over the past thirty days for every person requesting an upgrade. A recent unfulfilled request for an upgrade is worth one point; a weather delay is worth two points whereas a mechanical delay three points. A cancelled flight for any reason is worth seven. Add in a point value for status level (e.g., Platinum or Gold) and each of the requests can now be ranked by their recent history score. Upgrades are given out in rank order until all are gone.

Note that no one has to do anything because the system takes care of the situation. That system, however, can be overridden by a gate agent when helping a customer re-book during a flight interruption; otherwise, no human action is required.

Recognize also that the Target example provides us with an example of how research analytics can become operational. Taking transactional data they already had in their customer records, they used discriminant analysis or hierarchical linear regression to calculate the probability that a certain series of purchases could predict whether or not a woman registered as pregnant on the birth registry. Then they ran a series of experiments to confirm their original hypothesis and to fine-tune the model. Once they had the model, they made it operational.

Although a goal for research is to create better marketing operations, why do we include reporting analytics in this discussion? Why not focus simply on the research to operational link?

Two reasons. The first is probably obvious; reporting analytics create outputs that we watch to monitor operations. Reporting analytics provide managers with a simple view of a complex system. Think about Homer Simpson monitoring a nuclear power plant. If the light is green, all is ok. If it turns red, Springfield is in trouble. Behind those lights is a very complex piece of machinery but reporting analytics are converting that complex system into a simple reporting tool—green or red.

As our customers change and competitors adapt, our operational analytics can begin to tell us that our strategies are beginning to fail to yield the outcomes we desire. Monitoring outcomes through analytics gives marketers an opportunity to identify changes that signal a need for re-examination of our strategy and tactics. This process of organizational learning is illustrated in Exhibit 6.1.

The second reason for spotlighting reporting analytics is a bit more subtle. Reporting analytics requires resources. In a study we conducted of B2C firms, mostly retailers and consumer-packaged goods manufacturers, we observed that the resources (such as personnel and computer system time) used to create research analytics were often "stolen" from

Exhibit 6.1. An analytics-based process of organizational learning.

ANALYTICS FOR THE REST OF US   75

reporting analytics.[1] Data managers would turn off reports that seemed under-utilized and if no one noticed, the resources would be re-routed to research.

The **dependent variable** is the variable, the thing if you will, that we're trying to change or influence. In all forms of analytics, whether it be research, operational, or reporting, defining the right dependent variable both conceptually and operationally is critical. Some readers will be thinking at this point, "How hard can this be? All we want to do is influence sales!" Yes—and no. As Cabela's Phil Kaus noted, if we are tracking customer satisfaction because we think it is important for future sales to have satisfied customers now, then our operational definition of satisfaction had better be right because that's what our reporting analytics will be tracking. If that definition is wrong, then we will engage in activities to improve upon the wrong aspects of our business.

Let's take another example—a new product introduction. Sales are important to track—yes. But not all sales are created equal. Important questions to consider are such things as:

1. Which marketing element is spurring trial, or first-time purchase, and which is spurring repeat purchase?
2. Are consumers paying full price? If so, which consumers? If not, how much of a discount is required and is it necessary to discount to get trial or repeat purchase or both?
3. What is the frequency of repeat purchase, or length of the repeat purchase cycle? What proportion of first-time buyers are becoming repeat purchasers?

All of these questions require the same variable—sales—but not the same. All are important to the long-term health of the new product but specifying the right dependent variable and setting up the reporting analytics to track the right variable(s) is incredibly important to the manager of that new product.

Types of Data

In the previous chapter, you learned about the importance of accuracy and precision, two important characteristics of good data. There are other important characteristics of data that you've probably learned about in a statistics class but are worth pointing out here.

Numbers can sometimes mean different things to different people, and different things at different times. If I ask you to rank something, from one to ten, you will give me a number. Let's say I ask you rank 10 apples on the basis of tartness, from the least to the most tart. You rank a Granny Smith apple as number 8 out of the 10 apples you were given. I ask your partner to rate, on a scale of 1 to 10 from not very tart to very tart, those same apples. Your partner rates the Granny Smith as an 8. Is that the same thing? Is it the same as saying you have 8 apples?

On the face of it, the last question seems rather silly. At the same time, it points out differences in the meaning of 8. If your partner rated a Granny Smith as an 8 and a Red Delicious as a 4, does it mean that the Red Delicious is half as tart? If you have 4 apples and your partner has 8, you do have half as many. That number has a different meaning than ranking. But even the ranking has a different meaning than does a rating. If I were the one rating, I might rate two apples as an 8 on the scale, but if forced to rank, I have to decide. So, which has the greater precision—ranking or rating?

If we're comparing two very similar apples, ranking has greater precision. But what about when there is a large difference in apple tartness? Rating may have greater precision.

Interesting. But does it matter? The difference matters twice.

The first time the difference between ranking and rating matters is when you are designing the question. How close do you think the items you want compared are? Are they similar or different? Are we trying to figure out how similar or how different,—or how much (as in do we have 8 apples)?

The second time the difference matters is when you are analyzing the data. My cousin once had a pair of bird dogs. One was great at finding birds, the other at retrieving. He'd say, "Between them, I've got one good dog." In that situation, an average of the two was wonderful. But say I'm bringing the ball down the soccer field and I shoot, only to see the ball bounce off the right post. I get my own rebound and shoot again, only to hit the left post. On average, I had a goal. Unfortunately, I still have a zero on the scoreboard. The point here is that there's a time when you can use averages and when you can't, and those times are determined by what type of data you have. If you have a ranking, you can't use averages; you can with a rating.

The challenge is that we don't always know how we plan to use the data when we design our measures or record our data. We may think we know, but then someone always asks a question during the analysis phase. Or someone comes back later with a new question and you want to use the data you already have. If we can answer most of the questions we're asking with the data we have, say 70%—80% then the study should be considered successful. Still, there are always those questions that come up later.

Since that is so often the case, the best principle is to always ask for the most precise data possible, which means you want to use data that allows for averages. We call this type of data **metric data** (ranking and categorical data are called **non-metric**) and by metric, we really just mean that the numbers can be used to logically create averages.

Your current research question may only require non-metric data. For example, we ran a field experiment involving mobile marketing strategies. We divided the stores where we tested the strategies into three categories; small, medium, and large. We did that on the basis of square footage; in other words, we converted metric into non-metric. However, we still had the metric if we needed it.

Perhaps a better example would be to consider which of the three promotion strategies pulled the most sales. But influencing your results could be competitive action. To measure competitive action, you could purchase from Nielsen or other tracking services the actual count of competitor commercials. Or you could simply ask each of your store managers to rate the competitive action as either heavy, moderate, or mild. To make these ratings similar across managers, you would want to provide

Type of data	Sample questions	Sample answer scale
Metric	How important is speed of service to you?	1 = Not at all important to 7 = Very Important
	How much do you agree or disagree with the following?	1 = Strongly agree to 7 = Strongly disagree
	How long is the waiting period?	Enter the actual minutes
	Would you recommend us to a friend?	1 = Yes, Definitely; 2 = Yes, Probably; 3 = No, Probably not; 4 = No, Definitely not
	How satisfied are you with our service?	1 = Completely satisfied to 4 = Not at all satisfied
	Store size	Actual square footage
	Store size	Actual sales
Non-Metric	Please rank the following 7 features of service.	Ranking 7 items from 1 being most important to 7 being least, and do not use a ranking twice
	How long is the waiting period?	Choose from: 1 = less than a minute; 2 = 1 to 3 minutes; 3 = 3 to 5 minutes; 4 = more than 5 minutes
	What is your gender?	Male/Female
	What is your age?	Check one: 18-25; 26-37; 38-49; 50-65; over 65
	Store Size	Small, Medium, Large

Exhibit 6.2. Sample measures for metric and non-metric data.

them with definitions and with examples of what heavy, moderate, and mild look like, but even so, you may lose a little precision.

Distribution

Another factor to consider is the **distribution** of the data, or how a lot of observations for a particular variable are arrayed along its range. As students, we'd often ask our professors for a curve, thinking that getting graded on a curve would mean we would all get our grades raised. Actually, grading on a curve means that the final result is a **normal distribution**, a bell curve, which means that some grades might go up but just as many might go down. Two students getting an A means that two should also get an F and the average might be a 75—not what we were hoping for!

Mode is an important characteristic of a distribution as it is the point in the distribution with the greatest frequency. If most of the students made an 80, then that is the mode, even if the average is 78 (thanks to the one kid who made a 54 and pulled the average down). In a normal distribution, mode and mean will be near each other. But in some distributions, such as bi-modal which has two different but (nearly) equal modes, mode and mean can be very different. A distribution with a mode near one end or the other is considered **skewed**.

Distribution is important to consider. More astute marketers are finding that marketing to smaller parts of the distribution can be quite profitable, even though around the mode or mean may be the biggest segment. For example, the highest frequency users may be the best segment to target, or it may be that there is another segment that is willing to pay a premium for better than average service, even though they are less frequent users. Marketing to the average is not what dynamic marketing is about—but all of this so-called one-to-one marketing is still marketing to groups; it's just that we take smaller and smaller portions of the distribution and segment more tightly.

Further, remember earlier when we converted store size from metric (square footage) to non-metric (small, medium, or large). We may not have a normal distribution of store size, but if we convert it to groups, then we can create groups of equal size, large enough to help us find differences.

What you've read about so far is a form of data that is structured; or at least, the examples are structured. One of the challenges to using Big Data is that so much of the data we want to use are unstructured—at least when we get it. Let's take a look at what it means to gather and use unstructured data.

Unstructured Data

The term *unstructured data* is a bit misleading because there is usually some structure in place. Typically, when data scientists refer to **unstructured data**, they mean data that are received without an a priori data definition. Structure is the definition, the meaning assigned to various numbers. Rank and rating, for example, are two forms of structure used to create numeric data.

Examples of unstructured data include text data (such as from the Notes section of your sales force's customer records), images (such as photos), audio files (such as phone conversations recorded in a call center), and video (such as consumer path observation in a retail store). If you think about text or audio, the basic unit of data is words, used in a language and setting that provides definition. That's why we say that the term can be a bit misleading—there is a structure, it's just not a numeric structure.

The challenge, then, is to convert that structure into a numeric structure that can be analyzed and understood. If consumers are talking about a product, for example, words that indicate dissatisfaction can be scored as a negative number, praise for the product as a positive number. Further, superlatives can receive higher numbers compared to modest praise (or criticism). This form of bringing structure to text is the beginning of the process of **text analytics**, the process of analyzing and understanding text whether originally written (such as chat or email or resume data) or spoken (such as a recorded phone call).

Unstructured data remain one of Big Data's challenges and frankly a huge barrier to ROI—s or, depending on your view of the glass, one of Big Data's greatest opportunities. First, a high degree of creativity is needed to begin to think about what unstructured data might make sense to consider. For example, can we segment our market based on the types of people they are hiring? Or even the numbers? We can pull that data off the web and maybe consider the relative numbers of new positions as a measure of growth for forecasting purposes. I'm not saying that if you are in B2B, this is a form of analysis you should consider. But one has to wonder if there are really useful ways to look at the data that are there if we only knew which data to use.

Case Study: Gilt Groupe

Gilt Groupe is an aspirational retailer, meaning that they sell products that reflect upscale lifestyles at lower prices to people who aspire to live those upscale lifestyles. Strictly an online retailer, the company still communicates with customers via multiple channels, including email and chat. Further, because so much communication is digital and the data are streaming (that is, continuously coming in—remember Velocity is one of the Big Data characteristics), the company really needed to be able to create operational analytics that enabled the use of unstructured data.

By combining text data from emails and other direct communication with the consumer but also including Twitter and other indirect communication, the company uses text analytics to conduct sentiment analysis on an ongoing basis. If you recall from Chapter 5, Sentiment analysis is a form of text analytics used to determine if the overall market attitude (or sentiment) is positive or negative and along what dimension (such as price, quality, performance). Gilt applies sentiment analysis to decisions on pricing, promotion, and product. Everyone hates it? Sell it at half off. Everyone loves it? Order more and make it the first product they see.

But that's not all. With the Teradata Aster platform for managing the unstructured data, Gilt Groupe is also able to obtain streaming insight into segmentation. Using research analytics, they created clusters of consumers based on data from a wide array of sources, both structured and unstructured, including transactional data, browsing data, and text. Operational analytics then use pattern recognition to apply these segments to live data and consumers are dynamically presented offers appropriate to their segment.

Exhibit 6.3 illustrates how the company begins with data from a variety of sources to study. Segmentation studies and sentiment studies then result in two parallel processes. One process categorizes consumers based on their behavior and other learned variables (including demographics). The other process categorizes products based on consumer reactions. These two processes then combine to create offers matched to the segment.

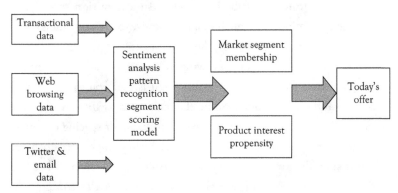

Exhibit 6.3. From data to insight to offer: Gilt groupe's process.

Applications to Marketing

The Gilt Groupe story provides a great example of how research analytics become operational, then reporting. That process is helpful in some instances; in other situations, there may not be a direct flow resulting in reporting analytics. To think about how analytics might be used is to think about what questions need answering by marketing, questions such as:

- Which promotion method or channel pulls best?
- How much budget should I allocate to a particular promotion strategy?
- What is the proper product assortment?

The answer to the first question seems easy: just look at the sales figures, right? Or maybe the answer is in traffic—which channel has the greatest traffic? But asking the question in that manner makes the assumption that the channel is operating independently of all others. In reality, we all know that consumers are receiving messages from us in many ways: email, direct mail, television commercials, on our website, as a banner ad, or a pop-up on an iPhone app. And whereas back in the day of three networks on TV, it was possible to operate under the principle that a consumer needed three exposures to an ad before there was an effect, the proliferation of commercial messaging is so great that it might require a dozen or more touches before we see any influence. How, then, do we determine how much effect each channel has?

If we can track a consumer all the way through the path to the purchase, we can create an attribution model. An **attribution model** is a model that determines how much weight exposure to a specific message or through a specific channel had on the final outcome. Although still in its infancy, attribution modeling is growing in importance as a decision aid.

Recognize that an important requirement is that you can track that consumer all the way through. Some channels, such as TV viewing, may not allow for tracking. Estimates based on **pulsing**, or spacing commercials, can be created—if behavior is modified during a high intensity burst of advertising, then we can assume the difference in behavior is because of the advertising, assuming we also hold everything else constant. In general, we're trying to see what works.

What defines "works," though, may vary. For example, if we have a situation involving a B2B sale that lasts a long time, we may want to identify key buyer behaviors along the path and then create attribution models that predict those behaviors. You may want to create a model that considers the relative importance of marketing variables that lead to an initial sales call, to a proposal, and/or to a demonstration. Each of those steps in the sales process are indications that the account is getting closer to purchase and are important intermediate outcomes.

How does the consumer interact with us? Using web browsing data, we can examine their online behavior. With smart antennae, we can track their shopping patterns in a store, as well as how much time they spend looking at a particular display, called **dwell time**. With small cameras, we can even track their eye movements to see what it is that caught and held their attention.

Sequential basket analysis of online transaction data also gives us insight into what is likely to lead to a transaction and what is not. Amazon may have perfected basket analysis in the form of "people who bought *this* also bought *that*" but it was Cabela's who first understood that if someone puts *this* in the basket, they're not only more likely to buy *that*, they're also more likely to actually purchase, and that you can use that product sequentialing in your offers to drive transactions at higher margins.

These are just a few examples of the types of analysis being done with Big Data. Each started out as a question—How do I select channels better? Which products should I promote? With the right data, each can be answered through analytics, and when possible, converted into operational processes that yield strong performance.

The utilization of customer insights to position merchandising strategy—not anecdotal, not vendor stories, but how do customers engage in your product to strengthen. Fill the need with your core buyer, the fringe will follow.

Summary

Analytics starts with good data—the right data. Research analytics involve the application of statistics to study questions, while operational or production analytics allow us to automate marketing. Reporting analytics then provide decision makers simple views of complex systems to track performance. All of these require the right data.

We prefer metric data, those that have averages that really mean something. Still, there are times when categorical, or non-metric, data are useful. Unstructured data is data, such as text, that occurs without obvious numeric structure and the first challenge is to give that data a numeric structure. One big opportunity in Big Data lies in finding unique and creative ways to structure unstructured data.

Market basket analysis is one of the earliest applications of operational analytics and is accomplished through affinity analysis. Attribution modeling is currently an area of tremendous opportunity in understanding the relative value of our marketing efforts. As mobile marketing and other forms of data collection take off, new types of analytics will be possible through research that will influence dynamic marketing into the future.

Discussion Questions

1. Describe a business example where unstructured or seemingly unrelated data would be useful. What data would you want and how would you use it?
2. Assuming you run a luxury hotel, what are three important questions you'd like to ask customers to really understand their level of satisfaction with your hotel? If your hotel was a value property (meaning low price), what three questions would you ask?
3. What is the most important lesson in the Gilt Groupe case study? Why is that the most important lesson?

CHAPTER 7

Turning Models Into Customers

Living in the Past is a Jethro Tull album, not a smart poker strategy.
—Richard Roeper

Introduction

You may not be familiar with either Jethro Tull, a rock band from the '70s and '80s or Richard Roeper, an apparent poker player, but living in the past is poor strategy indeed. Yet our models, without getting too philosophical, always represent the past because all of our data represent events that have already happened. How, then, can we take what we know and turn it into cash right now? To accomplish that objective, you have to be able to:

- Simplify your models for human operational use
- Create seamless customer conversations
- Convert those conversations into transactions, preferably without giving up margin

Simplifying Models

The beauty of human interaction is how adjustments are made on the fly. The human brain can process around 800 words per minute, yet the average rate of speech is only 120 words per minute. If we're tuned into the conversation, we have excess processing capacity vis-à-vis the spoken element that we use to process non-verbals such as posture, gestures, eyes, and many other elements to arrive at understanding.

Essentially, our operational models do the same thing. They process a lot of data to arrive at understanding, then use that understanding to respond.

One challenge is that we want our operational models to be useful to our frontline personnel. So our model of customer lifetime value (CLV) that we use to determine which offers to make and when becomes simplified into Gold or Platinum members. When I walk up to the ticket counter at American, they know very quickly that I'm a Platinum flyer and what that means in terms of CLV. Loyalty program levels are one way that we can simplify a model, though to be perfectly frank, few organizations think about it that way. If they did, they might add a layer or two of information.

What information would you want to add? It might help to know that I'm a million mile flyer, because loyalty program status (Gold, Platinum, Executive Platinum) is only what is happening this year. Whatever I did last year doesn't count; whatever I may do next year is unknown. Therefore, it might help to add that I'm a million mile flyer because that means I have a history with the airline, while this year's Platinum flyer is flying a lot right now. Both are valuable, they are just different. Far more valuable, though, would be to have an understanding of who I am, why I fly, and what I like.

To accomplish the more complete picture, companies develop **personas**, or humanized descriptions of customer segments that might include demographic information, motivational, and psychographic data, and other variables that more accurately communicate the nature of that customer.

Let's say you are Ping, the golf club manufacturer. You may be able to lump all of your customers into three broad categories, or personas, based on how and why they golf. These categories might be:

Bill & Betty Member are the couple or the person who plays weekly in a league whether it be a senior league, a women's league, or some other league. If married, they both play and regularly play together, as well as separately with friends. He or she generally plays with the same larger group of people, though foursomes will vary from week to week. Score is important so occasional lessons and regular practice sessions are part of the experience, but camaraderie is also important. This person will hang around the clubhouse after a round and while probably retired, may also work a schedule that allows for regular play, and will watch golf tournaments on TV.

Johnny Gambler plays regularly, probably once a week at the same time, with the same foursome. He or she is not as competitive as the league player but plays more often, is either retired or works shift work so he can play regularly, and never practices. Gambling is likely to be a part of his game, and is probably more important than his actual score. He will buy new clubs, shoes, and apparel every year but it may just be a new putter, wedge, driver, or bag. He keeps up with the pro tour and will watch golf or read about golf if given the opportunity.

Jack Bear is an avid golfer (the name is a nod to one of the game's greats, Jack Nicklaus, the Golden Bear) who also plays regularly, is likely to be a male in his thirties or forties, plays with friends on the weekend, and takes golf vacations. He watches the golf channel for shows on how to improve his game, reads *Golf* magazine, practices at least once a week, and buys new clubs at least annually. A regular charity tournament player, he will likely become a league player later in life and will compete for the championship. His wardrobe consists of golf shirts with embroidered course logos from his golf vacations.

Go back over the previous three paragraphs. What distinguishes one persona from another? Persona is a concept that has to be operationalized; that is, you have to have operational measures so that each customer can be identified appropriately. Otherwise, the company can't act on the concept.

While there are likely to be other segments, creating these three broad personas help Ping in many ways (note that Ping may actually have five or six segments; there's nothing magic about three). First, you can see how CLV is inherently part of the persona, but you can also see how motivations and the desired golf experience are also communicated within Ping by simply referring to the persona. When marketing decisions are being made, these personas are useful when deciding how to create messaging. "Let's create a golf school vacation package for the Members!"

You may be thinking, "Wait a minute—I thought one of the promises of Dynamic Customer Strategy (DCS) is to optimize the customer experience for each individual. Three segments are not individual experiences!" And you'd be right.

Two aspects of Personas bear discussing. The first is that these are broad categories driven by the data and designed to represent the market for ease in communication, understanding and decision making. Ping, for example, could decide to offer a Ping Golf School targeted toward the Members. The Members' persona would then drive the decisions about what the school would teach, how it would be priced and communicated, and so forth. As Ping marketers discussed the new school, all would know what it means to target Members.

The second aspect is that once those big decisions were made (such as which persona to target and with what), DCS would again come into play, and it would do so in two ways. The first way is to test those big decisions and make adjustments on the fly. Recall the case study of *Defending Jacob* and Random House in Chapter 4, where they positioned their marketing to target one market, then learned that the book really resonated more strongly with another market. That was **market-level DCS,** or the application of DCS to making decisions about the marketing mix of product, pricing, promotion, and distribution (or place, if you remember your 4 Ps of marketing).

The second way is that operational models would then enable the customer to customize the purchase experience, and to co-create the desired school experience. In other words, the individual still gets his or her way, still receives individualized attention, still co-creates that personal experience. That is **customer-level DCS**, or the application of DCS to create an individualized customer experience. Amazon's "People who bought this also bought that" offer is a simple example of customer-level DCS; a more complicated version might be Kroger's ability to determine if you are about to run out of toilet paper at home (based on their record of your past purchases and household size) and as you walk past the paper products aisle, they send a reminder "Don't forget toilet paper!" to your phone.

Conversation Mapping

Those two examples, Amazon and Kroger, represent making an offer in what James Cash Penney called "the last three feet," or that critical point at which the customer is in front of the product and either decides to buy or pass. But the customer conversation started well before that.

Customer-level DCS is about learning in the moment and responding accordingly. For many marketers, customer communication is all too often treated as a one-off event and one-way to boot. Instead, consider customer conversations as a form of decision tree, mapped to match the customer's decision process.

That decision process was, for centuries, mapped to four stages (sometimes five). The model, illustrated in Exhibit 7.1, is comprised of four stages that each person has to move through to get persuaded: Attention, Interest, Desire, and Action (sometimes Conviction is placed between Desire and Action). What few realize is that this model was first expressed by Aristotle as a framework for understanding how rhetoric works in persuading large audiences. The model fits well when a politician seeks to introduce a new piece of legislation, but it has limited value in understanding consumer decision making.

Since Aristotle, a number of scholars have created models that more closely approximate how consumers and organizations make buying decisions. Because entire books have been written on that topic alone, I offer a reading list at the end of this chapter should you want to follow that topic up (and I recommend that you do).

The key point for here is that your customer conversation should aid the consumer in making a decision. Selling the way the customer wants to buy is one way to gain competitive advantage.

A simple example is Lifesavers. Edward John Noble bought the Lifesaver Co. about a hundred years ago and began placing Lifesavers next to cash registers everywhere. Pricing the candy at a nickel, he encouraged cashiers to include nickels in change, thereby increasing the likelihood of an impulse purchase. As they say, the rest is history—and perhaps ancient

Action

Desire

Interest

Attention

Exhibit 7.1. Aristotle's model of persuasion.

history. Impulse purchases of products next to the cash register have substantially declined because we're on our phones as we wait to check out and we're not paying any attention to those little Pep-O-Mints begging to be bought!

But the point is that Noble matched how consumers would buy that product and made it easy for them to buy.

If there is one truism in marketing, it's that there is competitive advantage to be gained in selling the way the customer wants to buy. Yes, I did say that already, but it bears repeating. Amazon exists because the internet allows buyers to buy the way they want to—in their pajamas at three a.m. if they want.

In general, the decision to purchase is thought to be like any other decision. There is a gap between the current state and the desired state. The decision is made that the gap can be filled by a product or service.

Needs are then specified and translated into features. Based on those features, the buyer searches for products and then evaluates them. Included in that evaluation are characteristics of the vendor—reputation for quality, service, and so forth. Then a product is selected, purchased, and used.

While this model looks very rational and cognitive, we all know that many purchases are anything but rational. The purchase of an engagement ring; buying a convertible; selecting a vacation home—we may

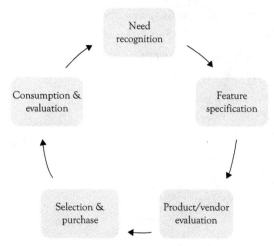

Exhibit 7.2. Purchase/Consumption cycle.

use rational thinking to evaluate features but the decision of which features are important may be highly emotional in origin. Don't get hung up in trying to find examples that don't fit the model; rather, focus on the nature in which one stage may be more or less important for some buyers in certain situations. If I'm buying Lifesavers, I may go from Need Recognition to Purchase without much feature specification (other than I like the various mint flavors over their fruit). If I'm buying something complex, I may spend a great deal of time in each stage, spending a lot of effort to make sure each of the small decisions is right.

The point here is that Big Data and DCS enable us to carry on an intelligent conversation with the customer as she or he moves through this process. In each stage, and from stage to stage, decisions are being made. What do I want? Why? How do I intend to use it? Will I consider your product? How will I consider it? All of these questions represent decisions, the little decisions that move buyers through the process and it's your job to give them the information they need to make the next decision.

Big Data offers the opportunity to operationalize insight—that is, as the data streams in, the operational systems analyze and respond accordingly, particularly at the consumer DCS level. The challenge is to create models that recognize the consumer's stage in the decision/consumption process and to create messages that respond accordingly.

When a customer engages with your organization, be it on the web or in a store, it pays to consider why they engage. Let's take a closer look at the interaction of streaming insight of the market versus consumer level by considering what a bank in Malaysia does.

Case Study: Maybank

In Kuala Lumpur, Malaysia, banking is extremely competitive, much like it is anywhere else. Products can be quickly copied and there is always someone willing to provide a service for a lower cost. Such an environment can quickly devolve to competing based on convenience or some other form of low value-adding feature.

What Maybank does, though, is different. Recall in Chapter Six we discussed the use of analytics for discovery. Maybank, because they've built a customer data warehouse (using the Teradata platform) that combined sources of data to provide a single view of the customer, are able to use their customer dataset to discover patterns in purchasing. This discovery process enables them to develop new products and services at a much faster rate. Although products can be copied, other banks are always behind the curve. This continuous development process creates a brand image, positioning Maybank in the minds of the consumer as *the* bank that is first to serve needs best.

Also important, though, is that they then apply marketing automation to communicate with customers. The classic example is the depositor who suddenly deposits a lump sum three times larger than normal. In many situations, this deposit is simply a pass-through; the sum is college tuition, for example. The customer could, however, benefit from a college loan or a college savings plan. A call from the customer's bank officer may identify the need and enable the customer to enjoy the benefits of a service that is more closely aligned with the need. This example is called **event marketing**; that is, an event triggers a marketing sequence. In this example, the event is the large deposit; in the Target case, the event is becoming pregnant. (Don't get confused with event marketing based on events like the Super Bowl.)

Thus, not only is Maybank using streaming insight to continuously develop new products, it is also using streaming insight to respond appropriately to a customer's behavior. This combination of market-level and customer-level DCS is what gives Maybank its unique competitive leverage.

Offers and Margins

An important point to recognize about the Maybank case, and virtually every other effective use of DCS, is that DCS enables organizations to make offers that leverage customer needs and desires, not price. Kroger texting a reminder to buy toilet paper doesn't mean that Kroger has to give a coupon to spur the sale. Maybank responding to a customer's deposit doesn't require an offer of a margin-eating special deal to win the business. Both simply require being in those last three feet with the right offer.

Discovery (recall that discovery is the application of analytics to historical data in order to understand the market) is important to determining those needs, wants, and desires, and plays a role in two ways. As noted earlier, selling the way the buyer wants to buy is one way to gain competitive leverage. Discovery can assist in understanding the purchase process by studying the sequence of events leading to a sale. Discovery can also assist in understanding how the product or service is consumed, to determine what needs and desires are being met. For example, Overstock.com can examine transaction composition of each buyer and identify which buyers use Overstock for complete wardrobe purchases and which use Overstock to fill in their wardrobe. Further, by considering what type of wardrobe, the company may be able to determine something of the buyer's lifestyle. For example, a complete lack of professional clothing may signal a stay-at-home mom or someone who works in a field not requiring that wardrobe. By making a few offers and seeing what the buyer responds to, Overstock can then narrow down the buyer's category. This narrowing then enables the company to make offers that are more targeted to the buyer's motivation for buying.

Did you notice the experiment in the previous example? Customer conversation is trial-and-error, trial-and-success, a series of experiments by which you learn about the customer. Recall the concept of progressive profiling examined in Chapter 5. As we carry out this conversation, we learn more about the customer and that enables us to make better offers, learning still more.

Finally, as marketing communications are created, such as a web page, a white paper, or a TV commercial, thought has to be given to what role that communication plays in the process of moving the customer through the decision cycle. In advertising terms, this is called the **call to action**; what action do you want the customer to take as a result of having received the communication?

The result is **cascading campaign** such as is illustrated in Exhibit 7.3, or a campaign that results in multiple paths to purchase.

As you can see, mapping the decision process of the customer aligns with mapping the marketing communication process. Each message is then a trial, and if the customer does what we hope, success! If not, error, but then our system may move that customer into a different group and a new sequence, or it may call for another message designed to re-enter the

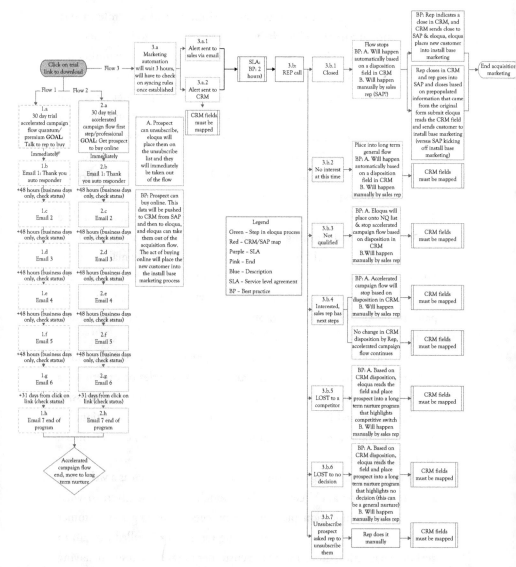

Exhibit 7.3. This flowchart illustrates an actual marketing campaign executed by the pedowitz group.

Source: The Pedowitz Group, used with permission.

process. As you can see in the exhibit, a "No" (at point A) to the first email may result in sending a different email leading into the same final offer, whereas a "No" (at point B) to the final offer may lead to the inference that the customer belongs in a different micro-segment.

Test and Learn

Once we put analytics into production and begin to operate using the campaign, the system can run itself. Test and learn becomes testing what type of buyer we are working with (is this person Betty Member or Jack Bear?) so that the right offer can be made.

At the same time, though, we are also testing the relative effectiveness of each message in the conversation. **Conversion** is the rate at which buyers move to the next stage. As we monitor conversion, we may find that one offer isn't doing as well. At that point, test and learn becomes testing to find out what will work better. Or it may be that we are launching a new product or program, in which case testing is needed to determine which messages should become operational.

Attribution Modeling

While message content is one aspect requiring testing, another is simply the **mode of communication**, or the channel by which the message is delivered. For example, mode could be a TV commercial, a web page, an email, or a salesperson. As we mentioned in the previous chapter, attribution modeling is an application of general linear modeling (of which regression is one form) to determine the relative value of modality or even a specific message. Attribution modeling allows you to determine how much weight to attribute to each message and/or mode in contributing to the final sale or series of sales. For example, suppose you are trying to allocate your marketing budget for the coming year. How much should be spent on emails, how much on white papers, how much on trade shows? If you can successfully determine the value of each mode, you can use that information to make sure you have allocated enough to each.

A challenge to attribution modeling is that most organizations fail to close the loop. Refer back to Exhibit 7.3. If a consumer visits your store but doesn't buy until later (perhaps over the web), how will you know? You can't close the loop.

Similarly, in situations where salespeople are responsible for making the sale, there is often an antipathy between sales and marketing which inhibits the ability to close the loop. Marketing may provide leads but never know what happens to them. As a consequence, marketing can't tell the relative value between trade shows and web-based marketing; for example, because there's no data provided back to tell whether customers were seen at the show or only visited the website.

You might assume that such a problem would be limited to smaller companies that use salespeople. However, we observed within a Fortune 5 organization (and no, the zeroes are not missing—that's Fortune 5, not Fortune 500) a major operating company that had no worthwhile data from salespeople in the CRM system.

If you think about this situation for a moment, you may suggest that the company simply take the list of companies that buy and compare it to the list of leads from marketing and see which leads purchased. But so much information is lost. For example, if a lead found via trade shows closes (buys) after two more sales calls whereas a lead found via web-marketing closes after four more sales calls, then there is a large value advantage in trade show leads.

Further, if you think about your last major complex purchase, you probably spent some time on the web, may have visited a number of businesses selling that product, and may have even sought other sources. Each contributed to the sale—but how much?

Attribution modeling can only be accomplished when we can identify who was where, when they were there, and what they did. We can do that for some customers, usually enough to draw worthwhile values for each mode and perhaps different message strategies.

Multi-Factorial Experimental Design

Another way to test and learn is through experimentation, a subject discussed throughout the book. Yet when we are testing messaging strategies, the situation is far more complicated than one might think. Many components, or factors, may need to be tested. For example, if you are testing an email campaign, you may want to test all of the following:

- Subject line—should it refer to a sale, or to a new product, or something else entirely?

- Opening line—should it be a salutation (Dear Karen), or an attention-getter (Sale Ends Saturday!), or...? And if it is an attention-getter, what's the right one?
- Product order—which goes on the left, which goes on the right? Which gets left out and which gets put in?
- Price?

And that's before you even think about which customer type or types are best suited, when the email should be sent, and a number of other questions.

If you **A/B tested** everything—that is, you only test two versions (A and B) of one factor at a time—you can see that it would take a very long time before you determined what actually worked. Of course, by then, it may be too late—your competitors may have blown right by.

Recall the concept of control from Chapter 2. Experimental control means that you take everything that you don't want to test and hold those constant, manipulating only the component you do want to test. If you want to test price, then hold everything else constant and only vary price. But how do you hold customers constant between the groups? If you send the higher value customers the higher price option, they may be more likely to pay for it but was it the price or the customer segment that caused the difference? By using **random assignment**, randomly selecting customers and assigning them to one group or the other, then the two groups should be equivalent. In this manner, bias or an erroneous result due to one group being different from the other is avoided.

Random assignment solves only one challenge. Another challenge is that if you tested all of those components listed above (subject line, opening line, product order, and price) at the same time with simple A/B testing, you wouldn't know which factor had the most impact on sales. The effects may have been due to price or product order or even an interaction of the two. Identifying which is more important or more influential will take more than an analysis of variance model.

Multi-factorial designs enable testing multiple variables simultaneously, and with far more levels than just two. Starting with a simple two-factor design and with two levels for each factor, there are four sub-groups. For example, if we are testing two pricing levels and two product presentation orders, then there are four groups. One group gets the low price and the shoes presented first, the second group gets the low price but with shirts presented first, the third group sees shoes first but with the high price, and the last group also gets the high price but sees shirts first.

Add another treatment or condition, such as the subject line (assuming we're testing an email campaign) and we don't just add two groups. Rather, instead of four groups, we now have eight. As we add additional treatments, then the groups continue to multiply. And this is just assuming that we only have two levels for each factor—some might have three, four, or more levels. Now your experiment may have to include thousands of customers, which means that you have fewer available to make money with once you figure what combination actually does work best.

Several methods exist for reducing sample size without losing control or by creating bias. One method, Taguchi Block Design, can reduce the required sample size, as can d-optimal methods and fractional factorials. Statistical software like SAS can not only analyze results using these designs, they can also help design the study to begin with. The point here is that you don't have to sacrifice learning to the pace of A/B testing—you can test many factors simultaneously.

Multi-factorial designs are another area where you'll rely on your data scientist or statistician to help you. Just know that you can test a lot of variables simultaneously *if you design your study ahead of time to do so.*

Summary

DCS can be applied at the market level to make decisions about what we will do strategically; customer level DCS helps create a conversation with each individual prospective customer as they move through their decision process. Companies create personas to assist in making market level decisions. At the customer level, many small decisions are part of the big decision; small decisions such as what is really needed, how much will be spent, and so forth. At each point in the conversation, we've got to help convert that customer to the next step. For some complex purchases, each step may be more tedious and take more time than for simple buying decisions. To model these processes and determine appropriate modes of communication, companies apply attribution modeling. To determine what each message should be, multi-factorial experiments are designed.

Discussion Questions

1. Map out the sequence of decisions you made when making a large purchase, such as a car, a television, or even a phone. Use a decision that involved at least a moderate degree of information search before you bought (e.g., if you are so loyal to Apple you didn't consider an Android, don't use a cell phone as your example). What were some of the sources of information that you used in making each small decision along the way? How heavily did you lean on manufacturer-provided information versus third-party information? How easy was it to find the information you wanted?

2. Create three personas as if you worked at a bank. Describe each persona, giving it a name. What characteristics would distinguish each persona?

3. Diagram a communication strategy to sell credit cards that support the local United Way for one of the personas in #2.

CHAPTER 8

Of Metrics and Models

When people thought the Earth was flat, they were wrong. When people thought the Earth was spherical, they were wrong. But if you think that thinking the Earth is spherical is just as wrong as thinking the Earth is flat, then your view is wronger than both of them put together.

—Isaac Asimov

Introduction

Asimov's statement is a reminder that being right or being wrong is a matter of degree—that often the question isn't whether one is right or wrong but how right and how wrong. In this chapter, we explore how to answer the question of how right was your plan. Afterward, you should be able to:

- Determine appropriate methods for selecting and displaying data to monitor performance
- Create stronger decision rubrics using performance data
- Use performance data to improve operational models

One of the themes of this book is that strategy is about making choices and the power of Big Data lies in making informed choices. If you are bringing an array of choices to an exec, three questions will be asked:

1. How much will we make?
2. How fast?
3. At what cost?

The basic fundamentals of monitoring performance, then, are answering those three questions in real time.

Measures 101

To begin our exploration into the types of metrics used to monitor Big Data-based marketing, we first need to review metrics in general. Most of this is probably old hat but just to make sure, we'll start at the beginning.

In general, performance measures are concerned with one of two characteristics: efficiency and effectiveness. **Effectiveness** is how much of something was achieved, such as how much gross revenue or the average transaction in dollars. **Efficiency** is the ratio of outputs to inputs, or the ratio of performance to investment. Return on investment (ROI) is an example of an efficiency measure because it is a measure of how well an investment performed.

Efficiency is a standardized measure. By **standardized**, I mean the measure is made comparable to others with the same denominator—so for ROI, the return is made comparable to other investments, keeping in mind that ROI is really Return/Investments so investments is the denominator.

How efficiently is one store selling compared to another? Some measures would be sales per square foot, sales per average hourly labor cost (a measure of employee productivity), or sales per advertising dollar. Now you can compare large and small stores and make better decisions about how big a store to build, how to allocate marketing funds across stores, and maybe even who is the better manager.

How efficient is your web advertising? Some measures would be eyeballs per dollar spent (how many people saw the ad divided by the cost), transactions per dollar spent (an ROI measure), and so forth. Now you can compare two options even if the cost is twice that for one versus the other.

Think, too, about the three questions we posed earlier. Velocity, or how quickly we see returns, is a form of efficiency. If we operate in a business-to-business environment, we also want to track things like time-to-close, which is how long it takes to convert a lead into a customer. Similarly, no matter our market, we may want to track time-to-payback.

This metric is useful when we have a significant customer acquisition cost that may not be fully recovered on the first transaction. The question then is how quickly can we recover that cost? Put another way, how quickly do we begin to generate a profit on a new customer?

Effectiveness can also be compared in meaningful ways. In retailing, one such measure is same store sales, year over year. This comparison is used to examine organic growth, or in this case, growth that is due to something other than acquisitions or expansions. If McDonald's experiences a same store sales decline, this means that the market is either shrinking or moving to competitors. Thus, efficiency measures are not the only standardized measures. Effectiveness can be standardized, too.

Market share is another comparable, or standardized, effectiveness measure. In the case of McDonald's, if same store sales are declining but market share is holding steady, which of the two reasons given earlier explains the decline? A shrinking market is the answer because McDonald's did not lose share.

Share-of-wallet (SOW) is an effectiveness measure that, when converted to a percentage, can be compared across strategies, segments, and businesses. Frankly, SOW can be more important than market share because the cost-to-serve on larger customers should be lower as a percentage of sales, yielding greater profit.

Both types of measures, efficiency and effectiveness, are needed. First, you can't calculate an efficiency measure without an effectiveness outcome. You have to know return to determine ROI. That aside, too much focus on efficiency might mean foregoing good opportunities or squeezing investment down to the point where revenue shrinks. A focus on effectiveness only leads to over-investing in the wrong activity. The challenge is to maintain a balance that hits revenue targets while staying within budget.

Efficiency and effectiveness are two ways to consider outcomes. Outcomes, though, are also a function of inputs so in some instances, tracking gross levels of inputs is important. Keep in mind that an efficiency measure is an outcome divided by an input—such as sales per square foot. Space, or square feet, is the input; sales the outcome. While you probably aren't going to manipulate the number of square feet on a daily basis, you may manipulate labor hours in stores or want to know the number of sales calls being made to sell a new product or increase the number of emails being sent out or know the number of offers being made on Twitter. These are inputs you'd like to monitor because you want to manage them.

Yet input tracking is sometimes the last thing marketers think of. In a board meeting, I once heard the manufacturing VP say "We aren't making money on our biggest customer because we discount so much!" The reality was, though, that they had no idea if they were making money or not because they didn't have the ability to determine **cost-to-serve**, or how much it cost to take care of that customer. Since one of the most important decisions you make is how much to spend on activities, it makes sense to track those costs on a per activity basis. Otherwise, how can you determine the return on your investment?

Monitoring

In our study of retailers, it was not unusual to find data teams generating thousands of reports on a daily, weekly, and monthly basis. In many cases, the reason for a particular report was long forgotten. In fact, a common practice is to withhold some reports on a regular basis to see if anyone complains. If there are no complaints, the reports are dropped and the resources are re-assigned to other tasks.

On the one hand, daily operations constitute a form of constant experiment for which monitoring is the same as hypothesis testing. On the other hand, monitoring results differ from hypothesis testing in that there is no counterfactual hypothesis against which to compare. For that reason, all we can know and hope to know with some degree of accuracy is whether what we are doing is functioning.

To determine whether our systems are functioning properly, a discussion of Deming's Theory of Variation is helpful. First, think of your marketing operations as a machine. With your car, if you put in the proper fuel and if the machine is tuned properly, then you'll observe a certain miles per gallon (a measure of efficiency). With your marketing operations, if you feed it the proper customer data, you should observe a certain return on your investment.

Over time, you'll see that return vary somewhat. If the marketing operations are working properly and if the customer data driving those operations are meeting specifications, then that range of variance should be relatively tight (or narrow). In Exhibit 8.1, you can see the range of performance for a series of marketing campaigns that Ping might be running with the three personas we discussed in Chapter 7. As you can see, the tolerance range for each campaign varies because no two campaigns will yield the same variance.

The function of monitoring is to ensure that results are staying within that tolerance range. If something breaks, such as a link to a website, an observant monitor would notice that the system is out of tolerance and determine the cause. Making adjustments to the system so that it runs within the optimal tolerance range is known as **tuning** (sometimes, you'll see this referred to as *tweaking*).

Variance can also be due to two other factors. One is **random effects**, those minor variances in inputs and other factors that simply can't be controlled. Another cause is the **environment**, or all of those factors outside of your marketing system that will influence outcomes. The economy, the competitors, the government—all have an effect.

A fourth cause of variance is called **systematic** effects, or the change observed when a new system is put into effect. When you implement a new strategy, what you hope for is a situation where the new tolerance range is entirely better than the old one—obvious system effects. That's

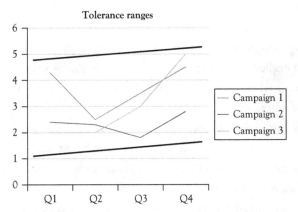

Exhibit 8.1. Tolerance range, or normal range of variation, is between the heavy dark lines for all campaigns. Note, however, that Campaign 2 has a significantly tighter tolerance range, ranging from a low of 1.8 to a high of 2.8.

not always the case, but as a general rule, we would not expect two marketing strategies to yield the same results.

The point is to not get too hung up on what is considered tuning the system or what is considered systematic effects. The point here is to recognize that there is an acceptable range of variance, called the **tolerance range**, and monitoring should be about making sure that systems are operating within tolerance. If not, then a closer examination should ask these questions:

- Is something broken? Or did someone "tune" the system and actually degrade its performance?
- Was there an environmental disturbance?
- Is this "machine" worn out and needs replacing?

If you stop and reflect on this reading, some questions probably come to your mind. The first should be how to determine the tolerance range.

A tolerance range is determined typically one of two ways. The first way is by executive fiat whereas the second involves statistics. Executive fiat methods typically involve setting only a minimum standard for performance and something that looks like this: "As long as we convert 10% of leads into sales, things are great. Fall below that and you're in trouble!" Executive fiat can be based on experience, a kind of personal experimentation that can prove valuable. Or it may simply be based on what is possible or it may be based on what is needed—that is, given a marketing budget, the bottom of the tolerance range is set at the conversion rate needed to hit sales targets. That's fine, too. Whatever the basis, you'll know whether it is reasonable by also determining the statistical tolerance range.

Look back at Exhibit 8.1 again. You can see the range—the range is simply the minimum and the maximum. But as we already know, the system sometimes breaks and the output falls below the minimum so how do you know what the minimum is?

First, let's assume a normal distribution of variance within the tolerance range. If that is the case, then three standard deviations in either direction should mean a significant change in performance. If your system yields a high volume of observations, the tolerance range created by simply looking three standard deviations below the mean should be sufficient. But if you have few observations (if you sell something with a long sales cycle and you don't sell that many), then you need something else.

Alternatively, your distribution may be skewed right—meaning that the mean is not in the middle of the range but rather near the top. That's often the case when you have a sales force, for example, that generally performs very well—most of them will have sales performance within a fairly narrow band if they are all using the same sales model and same quality of input. Given that the upper level is bounded by the capability of the system (the sales model or sales process) whereas the bottom is not (meaning you can only go up so far but you can fall all the way to zero), a skewed right data (or up, depending on how you display the data) is likely. In this instance, a statistically significant difference won't necessarily be three standard deviations below the mean. Rather, you have to adjust for the skewed distribution first but the principle is the same—you can set the lower bound of acceptable performance based on statistical significance.

What happens when the statistical range falls below an executive's comfort level? If executive fiat says 90% of the highest value is the bottom of the tolerance range and statistical analysis suggests it is 80%, what do you do? You only have a few choices. First, look for a better system—one that will yield 90% or better more regularly. That truly is your first choice. Your other choices are to try to change the mind of the exec, go through the motions of looking for causes to keep the system above 90%, and then look for a new job when you fail—because you will fail. No matter how hard you try, your Toyota Prius will not win the Daytona 500.

Visualization

Identifying the tolerance range is the second step in creating a monitoring system, the first being to decide what to monitor. The final step is to create a system of displaying the results so that monitoring can occur.

An important characteristic of visual data representation to keep in mind is that you are reducing data to two dimensions. In Exhibit 7.1, we reduced sales data to volume and time, the two dimensions. If we chose to illustrate that line graph as a bar chart, it is still just two dimensions. We could have done a pie chart (though that would be silly for the two dimensions we have selected, as each slice would represent one month) but the point is that even a pie chart is just two dimensions.

For this reason, **static displays**, or those visualization systems that generate a report without access to the underlying data, are becoming obsolete for monitoring purposes. For example, if you got a report on a piece of paper, all you have is what's on the paper—that's a static display. You may generate such a report for a meeting with the board of directors but it isn't their job to monitor daily outcomes, it's yours. You need something different, something that is not only up to the minute but that also gives you access to underlying data. If something is broken, you need to be able to find and fix it.

Real-time displays are those that allow the user to drill down into the data to understand more if needed, and provide up-to-the-minute (or thereabouts) data. You may need only daily updates but want the drill-down option, which still qualifies as real-time displays. The frequency of updating is optional but at least daily or you're really dealing with a static display.

Another way to think about visualization is to consider the graphic image you are creating. One way to think about graphic images is to use the Rand categorization.[1] This framework divides visual images into three categories: conventional, structured, and unstructured. **Conventional displays** use images with which we're already familiar, like bar charts, pie

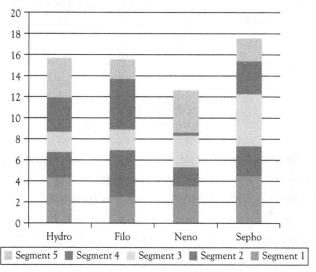

Exhibit 8.2. Conventional display of sales by segment & product type.

charts, and the like, as illustrated in Exhibit 8.2. In this display, you can see a bar chart representing sales for various product lines by customer segment.

Structured displays will use unconventional images but in patterns that make sense. An example is presented in Exhibit 8.3. This particular image is a pinwheel, and if your data were represented in this fashion, it might suggest an S-shaped distribution of sales within and across customer segments (the lighter portion of the pinwheel). Further, if this exhibit was a live display and not static, you could click on any area of the display and drill down to learn more. You are probably having difficulty interpreting the display and that's to be expected: Structured displays are best understood by viewers who are trained to understand that particular type of image. So if someone were using a pinwheel display, it would be because to that user it is like a conventional display; he or she is familiar enough with that type of image to understand and interpret it. The value, though, is that you can gain another dimension to the data. If you look at the pinwheel in Exhibit 8.3, you can see that it looks more like a

Exhibit 8.3. A structured display of sales across segments by product type.

3-D graphic. The three dimensions here are sales, customer segment, and a third variable that represents product type within segment.

Unstructured displays represent mathematical patterns as irregular spatial distributions. In Exhibit 8.4, we illustrate similar data but add the dimension of time. The x-axis represents time periods while the y or vertical axis represents average transaction. The blocks represent product categories. You can see the order in which products are purchased and the relative amount of purchase (width of the line) by segment. You could use the same display but instead of lines, represent customers as cars on a traffic grid. In this way, you could see where customers are in the purchase journey, for example, as an estimate of where they are in the customer lifetime patterns.

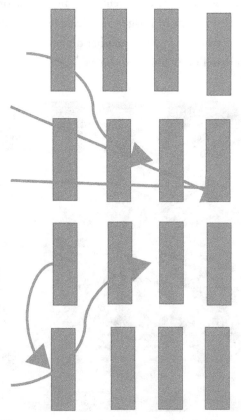

Exhibit 8.4. Unstructured display illustrating sales by segment and product in order and purchase size.

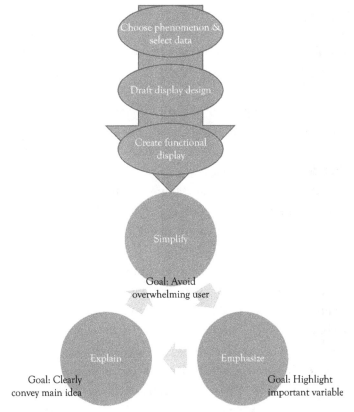

Exhibit 8.5. Display creation process.

Source: Adapted from Kornhauser, Wilensky, & Rand 2009.

When would you use any of these three illustrations? The first tells you relative value of each customer segment for each product. You may use this illustration to decide which segment is the most valuable for each product category and worthy of additional marketing effort or you may use it to identify where your marketing isn't working. The second illustration, the pinwheel, might be useful in breaking segments down into sub-segments (which part of the S-curve are they on and why?) or help you understand the variance in sales within a segment. The final illustration could be useful in helping you build models regarding what to offer and when in a customer's lifetime. You may also identify other ways to use these illustrations but the point is that you create the illustration based on the decision you need to make.

Further, it may be helpful to display the same data in different ways when trying to understand relationships among the variables. Visual displays should help you recognize patterns in the data more quickly. Exhibit 8.5 illustrates the process by which you should design and evaluate dynamic displays, beginning with deciding what it is you want to display and then iteratively simplifying to clarify what you intend to explain.

Finally, we distinguished earlier between static and dynamic displays, with dynamic meaning that the display is created with live data and you can drill down into the data to get a deeper meaning. Fully dynamic displays add two additional dimensions: real-time data and motion. For example, if you were viewing a display of last month's sales in Excel, you could click on the chart and look at the data. That's not very dynamic. More useful would be to be able to look at current data—to drill down into sales data that reflects today's activity. Even more useful would be to put that data into motion; that is, to view in motion how it changed from last month to now. Think of a weather map. You can see where the storm is now but you can also click on a link and put that map into motion. Now you can see how fast the storm is moving and in what direction. The same is true of a fully dynamic display, and you can do that with conventional, structured, and unstructured displays.

Popular Measures and Better Decision Rubrics

The purpose of monitoring performance is to improve performance—so obvious, why state it? It is because decision makers often focus on the performance and not on the improvement. In many instances, decisions can be improved by improving the monitoring and measurement processes.

Let's start first with assumptions. One important assumption often made is ceterus paribus—or all things are equal. Today is equivalent to yesterday and to a year ago. Yet the obvious difference between last year and this year is the economy. Between yesterday and today is the weather (which can have a major influence on Home Depot's sales and not influence Cabela's sales at all). Between 9/10 and 9/11...

You may find it entirely appropriate to act as though today is the same as a year ago as far as external factors are concerned. Just make that decision, don't let it get made for you.

Another assumption is the infinite time horizon. This assumption comes into play when calculating customer lifetime value. **Customer lifetime value** (CLV) is the sum of all future revenue from a customer, discounted to account for inflation back to today's dollars. I spent, in one year, $28,000 on air travel with American Airlines. If I flew at that rate every year for 10 years, I'm worth $280,000 gross to American but keep in mind that tomorrow's dollars are worth less because of inflation. Discount that total back to today. Further, you also have to keep in mind that American doesn't know what I spend on other airlines. My total CLV for airline travel has to include others, which American can only learn via a survey.

You can then sum the individual value of every customer and get a valuation of the company's worth. If the market value of the company's stock is less, then it is underpriced. Hedge funds and commercial bankers operating in the merger and acquisition market do exactly that to determine whether acquiring a company is worthwhile, though most companies use a proxy (such as whether I'm a Platinum frequent flyer). But the problem that has to be addressed is the length of a customer's life. If the acquisition will be held for 5 years, then the time horizon is 5 years. But what if the average customer life expectancy is 3 years and then they switch to a new provider? In that instance, ceteris paribus has to be applied in the hope that customer acquisition is at least as good into the future as it is now.

Similarly, you could assume ceteris paribus backward 5 years, using the **cohort and incubate** approach. The cohort and incubate approach begins with tracking the net present value of customers acquired in 1 year, 5 years ago (the cohort) to today. That tracking period is the incubation period. All things being equal, a cohort acquired 5 years ago should be the same as this year's cohort; if 5 years is the desired useful life then the value of that original cohort can be multiplied by five to get the total value of the firm's customers. Keep in mind, though, that total CLV (or total wallet size) can't be observed directly using cohort and incubate—it has to be gathered via survey, attendant with all of the potential sources of error that is part of surveying.

Several points are worthy of discussion. First, consider the challenges in revenue versus margin. Much easier is calculating gross CLV rather than net because you don't have to take into account varying costs. Alternatively, some experts hold that margin is more likely to remain relatively constant and should be used. Second, CLV can be calculated based on your company's share of wallet or the entire size of wallet. The choice is determined by the decision to be made.

Another commonly-used metric is Recency, Frequency, and Monetary (RFM) scoring, or RFM value. Consider questions such as at what point do you stop counting someone as a customer. A recency of purchase metric can answer that question for you. Then add in the frequency with which someone purchased, as well as how much was purchased. eBay considers a customer to be a customer if activity occurred in the previous 12 months; however, you could weight more recent purchases more heavily if you were trying to understand or monitor retention.

RFM scoring tells you more about a single customer right now than does CLV. Further, it is much easier to calculate and doesn't require estimation. For that reason, RFM is more popular, particularly in operational models, than CLV.

Advertising has a long history that influences metrics and monitoring. Currently, you hear people talk about eyeballs, but the concept goes back to how many people listened to the radio before there was TV, and how many people read a newspaper before that. **Impressions**, or the number of times an ad is viewed, is the beginning. Impressions is an outcome measure that can be standardized in a number of different ways. One way is by calculating **gross rating points**, or GRPs, which is the total impressions divided by the number of people in the audience. You might get a million impressions with one banner ad (or one tweet or one email) but that may only represent 100,000 unique people in your target audience. Most of those impressions were wasted (viewed by people out of your market). If you want to know how many people in your market viewed your ad, you want **reach**. Finally, **CPM**, or *cost per thousand*, then standardizes impressions to a CPM reached (and use per thousand in the desired audience, not total).

Yes, these metrics came from traditional advertising but the reality is that even today, these metrics are used to make decisions about whether to invest in a new mobile marketing app, digital signage, or web-based email campaigns. Their universality is what makes them popular. For example, **page views** is conceptually the same as impressions, as this is a measure of how many times the page was seen.

We mentioned the popular **Net Promoter Score**, NPS, which is the difference between the proportion of customers willing to recommend you and the proportion of customers who are unwilling to recommend you or even recommend that potential customers avoid you. Although some, such as Fred Reichheld the NPS inventor, argue that this metric is the single most important known to humankind, recent research suggests otherwise. Still, the measure is an important and popular measure of satisfaction. In addition to the limitation of having to gather it via survey (as with CLV), NPS suffers from the challenge of only identifying global satisfaction which may be of limited value.

For example, if you had a great time in Boston at the Marriott Copley, you may be willing to recommend it. But what about your friend's travel budget? Would that influence your willingness to recommend? Thus, one implicit assumption in NPS is that the buyer gives you a score for a certain consumption experience and not for others. If you assume that away, you may miss important opportunities. Or, that assumption may not matter because you've explicitly included it, either as a phrase in your survey ("In situations where budget doesn't matter, how likely would you be to recommend us?") or by understanding the situation in which the consumer used your hotel (e.g., you may have only surveyed business travelers).

I promised better decision rubrics and the first step to better decision rubrics is to know what assumptions lie at the foundation of your measures. We've only touched on a few. If you're faced with perplexing results, first consider the assumptions under which the data were gathered and check to make sure they match the assumptions of your decision. For example, if you're working on a business traveler problem, make sure your NPS was calculated using a business traveler sample. Sounds simple, but you'd be amazed at how often what seems simple is overlooked.

The second step is to design the measure to fit the decision; don't fit the decision to the available metric. Again, digging into ancient history, if all you have are impressions and you are trying to choose which radio station to advertise on, you can only choose the one with the biggest audience. But if you are trying to reach a Hispanic market, you may want to choose a smaller but targeted station. You won't do that, though, if you fit the decision to the data.

Finally, use statistics in your decision. Knowing the tolerance range is an example of how you can use statistics to detect real changes that are worthy of decisive action.

Case Study

Royal Bank of Canada (RBC) has long been touted as an innovator in the area of customer value analysis, but this 150 year old bank hasn't stopped there. The real break-through, though, started when the bank began to leverage Activity Based Cost accounting, an accounting approach that allows you to identify the actual cost of each activity. You can then apply that to the individual customer level by adding up the costs of all of the activities you engage in with each customer to derive a **cost-to-serve** value. The bank realized that cost-to-serve is only half the picture—there is also the actual individual revenue. When the bank identified actual revenue for each individual client instead of using average revenue for each product or average revenue for each client segment, they found that they misidentified the value of three out of four clients—and not by a little. Most of those clients jumped in value by three or more levels, meaning RBC had grossly underestimated these clients' value!

Cathy Burrows, RBC's Director of Strategic Initiatives and Infrastructure, says, "It's not just the calculation of a single number that is useful. We're able to drill down into each of the components that make up that number—direct and indirect expenses, for example. That richness of data really helps us understand what drives customer value."

If you stopped to think for a moment, you'd realize that these are the first steps to CLV—calculating the individual cost-to-serve and the individual revenue levels. But the bank didn't stop there. They are also beginning to track conversions. In today's online world, for example, you probably do a lot of your banking online, which is convenient for you and cheap for the bank. But the bank then loses the opportunity to engage in a face-to-face dialogue and learn from that deeper interaction. So in some cases, getting you to come in is an important outcome of a marketing interaction. By identifying which activities lead to an in-bank appointment, bank marketers can determine the relative value of each activity.

And it doesn't stop there. "What's important is having the framework (the conceptual map) to work against—are you measuring the right things, can you get the right data?" says Burrows. Without the fit between the operational and conceptual definitions, the metrics don't help you make the right decisions.

Summary

When execs want to know how well marketing programs work, they consider effectiveness and efficiency. They want to ask two questions: how much and how well. Answering how much, such as how much was sold, describes effectiveness. How well assets were used to generate those results satisfies the efficiency question. Examples of efficiency include ROI, sales per marketing dollar spent, and the like.

Because strategy is about making choices, comparing results from one strategy to those of another is important. Standardizing results allows for such comparisons. But even examining the effectiveness of a strategy over time requires some basis for comparison. Applying a tolerance range helps point to whether tuning is required or if a new strategy is needed.

Popular metrics, such as CLV, are based on certain assumptions that have to be specified to understand the limitations of the metric. The most important assumption to overcome is that you don't have a choice in metrics. Fit the metric to the decision, not the other way around.

Discussion Questions

1. What is more important, efficiency or effectiveness? Why?
2. How do companies get stuck in reporting ruts, generating reports that no one uses? What is the consequence to the marketing manager?
3. Go back to the Chapter 7 and the diagram of the campaign (Exhibit 7.3). List the top five most important metrics (from most important to least) you'd want to track if you launched this campaign and describe why those are the five most important.

CHAPTER 9

Making the Case for Big Data Solutions

Rounding off at the nearest cent is sufficiently accurate for practical purposes

—Alexander John Ellis

Introduction

Dynamic Customer Strategy (DCS) is a necessary set of skills and tools to maximize the return on Big Data. To obtain and develop the skills and tools takes investment, sometimes significant investment. That's why, at the end of this chapter, you should be able to

- understand how to quicken time to value (TTV);
- make a business case for Big Data tools;
- how to get the most from your technology;

In the previous chapter, we identified metrics useful in determining how well your marketing models are working. In this chapter, we dive into other metrics that are useful in examining your Big Data strategy, the technology purchase, and other similar decisions that are not tied to a single marketing strategy.

In early 2012, Gartner, a major consulting company in technology, predicted that the CMO would spend more on technology than the Chief Information or Chief Technology Officer by 2017.[1] Already, estimates are that marketing spends up to 45% of the company's technology budget. Although much of that hype depends on what you call marketing technology and downplays the role of the CIO unfairly, the reality is that marketing spends a lot of money on technology. Therefore, it just makes good sense to learn how to select technology. Further, it makes good sense to learn how to get the most out of technology.

Making the Business Case

Sometimes, making a decision seems so obvious, at least to the person proposing the change. Even so, decision makers need you to make a good business case for the specific proposal. Simply waving the Big Data flag in front of an executive is just as likely to cause a heart attack ("it will cost a fortune!") as it is to get your project or strategy funded.

Exhibit 9.1 identifies the elements needed in a business case, which is simply a form of a business proposal. The **business case** is the justification for making a decision, a decision that can include purchasing new

1. A brief, compelling, motivating statement—either a problem or an opportunity
   a. What opportunity exists for the organization to capture?
   b. How does this problem hinder achieving important goals?
2. A vision of the future when successful
   a. Integrate into an existing corporate conceptual map or strategic framework when possible
3. A description of the specific objectives to be achieved
4. A description and rationale for your preferred approach
   a. Include descriptions of the benefits for all relevant stakeholders
   b. Address relevant stakeholders' possible objections
5. Metrics used to evaluate the success of the initiative
6. A statement of the likely risks of your initiative and how they will be mitigated or eliminated
7. A basic plan of work with a timeline and key milestones
8. A project management plan and names and roles of key managers
9. Alternatives considered and how they would or would not work
10. Financial analysis
    o Cost estimates and potential sources of funding
    o Financial metrics, such as Return on Investment (ROI), payback, and so forth.

Exhibit 9.1. Elements of a business case.

technology, hiring new people, acquiring a company, or just about any other decision that the organization needs to make.

Most students are good at the first four parts and tend to leave out the rest. But consider your business case as a sales proposal and remember that it is likely to be read by a decision maker that you may not actually talk with. You need your business case to sell for you when you aren't there so it needs to be complete. You may also need someone else to implement all, or at least most, of the plan. Your business case will serve as the implementation guide.

Many students wonder if they should have at least ten sections with each section labeled as listed above. Perhaps. The proposal should cover all of those points but the depth required for each may not be enough for a simple proposal to require all ten as separate sections. Financial analysis will always be a separate labeled section, and there will always be a section at the start labeled something like Purpose or Goals or Vision. Or these may be slides in a presentation deck.

So what's different, then, about the Big Data business case from other business cases? It depends on the decision makers you are trying to convince and the culture in which you all operate. First, you have to assess whether your decision makers are comfortable with Big Data. Do they understand the value that can be derived? Have they funded similar initiatives? Do you have language and concepts (like personas) that help them navigate the complexities within Big Data? You may have to educate them.

Second, what's the strategic culture? If your organization has an integrated DCS approach, complete with conceptual maps, then you are halfway home. If they don't, then you have to craft a business case in the language they do understand. If you want to sell to the Chinese, you can't sell in Spanish. If you are selling your initiative to executives who understand finance better than they understand customers or marketing, then you'll have to present your case based entirely on financials. But if they understand DCS, then you can present it in terms of customer impact, customer lifetime value and the conceptual map.

Making the Financials Work

Funding a Big Data initiative is like any capital budgeting problem. Therefore, the decision arrives with the typical concerns. One concern is cash flow, which is related to TTV. **Time to value** (TTV is the amount time required to achieve the promised value. Since most Big Data initiatives generate revenue and don't just save money, the question that TTV tries to answer is how long will it take before we start generating cash at the promised rate? If you are proposing a solution that is supposed to add 5% to your monthly revenue, TTV would tell you how long it takes to achieve that 5% revenue growth. Note that, unlike pure cash flow, the metric is not about when you start generating positive cash flow. That's a separate and also important question, one that considers how long it takes before your cash inflow is greater than your cash outflow.

The most important metric in any capital purchase is ROI. The challenge, though, in any business case is identifying all of the return. The investment is fairly easy, though you need to know if your decision makers want you to include hard and soft investments. **Hard** investments or costs are those for which the company actually writes someone a check. This measure is the sum of all of the payments made to the various vendors needed to implement the proposed solution. **Soft** investments or soft costs are all of those operating costs needed to implement but absorbed by other, non-capital budgets, and include personnel time, travel costs if needed, lost production time during a cut-over (the time used to bring down the old system and bring up the new), and so forth. In some instances, management may want you to calculate ROI on hard and soft costs but you should also be able to include hard and soft return. Hard return is the real revenue gain and/or reduced vendor payments (for cancelled licensing fees, equipment no longer needed, etc.) whereas soft return is the value of non-cash items like increased employee productivity. In most instances, if you want to include soft returns you also have to include soft costs but the ultimate choice of whether to include soft costs and gains is likely be made by the decision maker, and in many instances, they want to see ROI calculated twice, once each way.

Typical capital budgeting metrics like payback will also be necessary. **Payback** is the time it takes for the return to equal the capital investment. Typically, payback involves hard costs and hard returns only because it involves getting the capital back so it can be used again. A similar measure is time to break even; except that this measures the time it takes for revenue to equal operating costs. Both of these are similar in concept to TTV in that the concern is how quickly will this decision to begin to pay off.

Calculating ROI in Big Data land can be difficult because of three questions. The first concerns the "before" picture you want to assess, because the chances are good that you don't have the right data. For example, if you want to show compressed sales cycles as a benefit of the new initiative, do you have the data to show how long sales cycles are now?

The second question concerns scoping the variables properly. This question is really more of a concern after the implementation and serves as a reminder that you have to create the proper metrics to fit the decisions you make, not make decisions based on what you have.

The final challenge: Can you quantify the benefits? A recent study by the Insight Technology Group claims these results, also shown in Exhibit 9.2, for customer-facing Big Data initiatives:

- Up to 42% revenue increase
- Up to 35% reduction in cost to sell
- Up to 25% reduction in sell cycle time
- An average 2% increase in margin
- An average 20% increase in customer satisfaction[2]

Can you cite these numbers for your proposal? Sure, the vendor selling you the solution will want to use these exact numbers as if they

Exhibit 9.2. Maximum gains observed for customer relationship management solutions.

Source: Adapted from Insight Technology Group.

were true for you. But these are either upper limits or averages—actual results will vary and vary greatly. In many instances, a decision maker may ask for best case, worst case, and most likely case scenarios, especially if quantifying the benefits means multiple new measures coupled with forecasts.

Selecting Technology

Selecting technology is likely to be a major part of any Big Data play. There are many resources that can help you with selecting a specific form of technology. Here, we want to focus on several factors.

First, prioritize which form of technology based on your strategy. There are many forms of technology that support DCS in Big Data. You may need analytics software, marketing automation software, or something else entirely, just as an example. What's likely is you may want many different technologies but prioritize based on what is likely to yield the greatest return on your strategy.

Second, as one of my business partners once said, you don't want to cut your foot to fit a new shoe. When selecting technology, you want to choose something that fits your people and your processes. If you need new processes, work on them but don't expect a technology choice to fix those problems. Instead, choose a technology that fits the people who will use it and the processes that you should have in place.

Bruce Culbert of the Pedowitz Group has been a part of many technology purchases as an independent consultant. When Bruce helps a client assess a technology, he considers several factors, including:

- Solution fit—how well does the proposed solution meet the specified needs, now and into the future?
- Culture fit—will the vendor's culture fit with the buyer's? Depending on the strategic importance of the purchase, this question can increase significantly.
- Track record—what is the vendor's track record in reliability, delivery, and all of those other factors that are not characteristics of the product itself? (Product characteristics are considered in solution fit.)

Paul Greenberg sees these first two factors as "Value and values for value and values." This statement reflects the fact that the value exchange has to be equitable—you have to get what you pay for. But more importantly, when something is strategically critical as Big Data is, there has to be a fit in the values of the two organizations. Otherwise, conflict will arise that can't be resolved. Sharing similar values means that both sides will approach challenges and opportunities in a similar fashion, making solutions more likely. Don't forget that whatever your choice, you'll have to live with it for a long time.

Pilot

In many instances, you may want to pilot the solution. Teradata, for example, offers customers pilots that can last up to six months. For a pilot to work properly, though, your organization has to make a commitment to trying it fairly. A good pilot has these characteristics:

- A commitment and budget to properly train personnel to operate with the new solution
- A commitment from the vendor to provide personnel to operate the new solution if needed
- Pre-set metrics that are well-defined and mutually agreed upon prior to the trial
- A specific time frame.

Any new solution represents change. Any resistance to change hurts the pilot, because the proposed solution is not given a fair shake. Commitment to the pilot has to be more than a pledge from a decision maker; commitment to the pilot has to be agreed to by all of those who will use the new solution so that they can personally manage the change, including their own feelings about the proposed change.

Further, the best pilots are those with clear and transparent decision criteria. The vendor and everyone in your organization know how the final decision will be made and the criteria that will be used to make it. Making a vendor and your team try to hit a moving target is demoralizing to your team and unfair to the vendor. Therefore, take the time up front to think through your decision criteria. Yes, things can change but try to avoid change because of a lack of up-front effort or care.

Getting the Most from Your Big Data Solution

Getting the most from Big Data first requires that everyone be on board. In the next chapter, we discuss how you build the right customer-focused culture that supports DCS, but even within the right organizational culture, you have to make sure that technology is used completely and correctly, that data get entered appropriately, and that processes are followed that enable sound DCS.

Securing Technology Compliance

One important factor in getting a Big Data proposal accepted and implemented is executive sponsorship. Someone at the top has to lead the charge, because adoption of Big Data technology is more than just a simple purchase of software. *Executive sponsorship* is necessary but by itself is insufficient.

Currently, we know of one customer relationship (CRM) manager in a B2B division of a major company who is afraid of losing her job because she can't perform. But she can't perform because she's incompetent. The problem is that the Division chief executive officer mandated the purchase of a CRM software system and hired her to run it, but then he left and the replacement didn't care. Salespeople who had to enter the necessary customer data to really power her solutions didn't cooperate. They couldn't see any personal value so they didn't enter the data; as a result, the lead generation solutions she came up with were less effective—so ineffective, in fact, that the salespeople wouldn't use the leads. If they

- Secure appropriate executive sponsorship
- Involve users in selection, design, and implementation
- Pilot
- Generate quick successes
- Communicate the strategy and the solution's role in the strategy
- Eliminate workarounds
- Align users' metrics and reward structures

Exhibit 9.3. Improving adoption of big data systems.

don't call on the leads, the leads don't become customers and the whole thing spirals into a black hole. Since she's afraid of the negative publicity, we can't share the name of the company but I'm certain you have some of their consumer products in your home right now.

When faced with adopting a system that will be used by a wide array of users, several important lessons can be learned from this example. The first is that one important set of users, salespeople didn't see the personal value so they failed to comply. One reason they couldn't see the value is that they didn't participate in the selection process, the design process, or the implementation process. As a result, a system was bought, built, and implemented that didn't deliver much value to them. Yes, they'd get better quality leads but that's only a small part of the potential value and the return on leads is historically so dismal that a new system isn't going to sell itself. *Involve users in the selection, design, and implementation.* You don't have to involve all of them but do have representatives that the rest of the users know and trust.

The second lesson learned here is that they failed to comply because they were allowed to not comply. If you need the cooperation and compliance of users for the system to work, the system has to be necessary for them to do their work. Therefore, *eliminate workarounds*. For example, salespeople have to complete and turn in reports like who they called on and what was the result, sales forecasts, and the like. A good CRM system eliminates those reports and allows the manager to pull the data directly from the system. When KMBS adopted CRM technology, salespeople were not allowed to turn in their own versions of reports created in Word or Excel so that they would have to use the system as intended (they also saw more value because they don't have to spend time creating reports).

Similarly, make sure that *users' metrics and evaluation/reward structures align* with proper use of the system. If people are rewarded to do something different, that's what they'll do.

Pilot the system and *generate quick successes*. First, a good pilot eliminates problems before it reaches the field. If a lot of users are going to be on the system, test and make sure all of the bugs are out before the system goes live for everyone. Most vendors will allow you to pilot the system anyway before you buy it and the pilot will enable you to validate that you'll generate the necessary ROI to make the purchase worthwhile.

Second, ensure that some quick successes happen to generate positive word-of-mouth among the users.

Finally, when rolling out the full system to the field, carefully *plan your launch strategy*. Your launch strategy should be comprised of three components: communication, training, and reward/punishment. The communication component should include messaging around why the system is important for the company, how it will benefit the user, and information on training and support. If you want **buy**-in, you need a communication strategy that **sells**. You also need training and support commensurate with the complexity of the system. Simple systems require less training and support; complex systems need more. As part of your launch strategy, you should also consider a series of early rewards that encourage trial. For example, you could have a contest with a small prize available to every user who completes 5 sessions in the software. Whatever it is, use rewards to encourage trial, not success. Success should already be rewarded in the normal evaluation and reward system—for example, salespeople get paid to sell. If the system helps them sell, they've already gotten that reward. Focus instead on the desired activity, such as entering data. Similarly, and tied to eliminating work-arounds, devise appropriate punishments if they fail to comply. If someone hasn't logged into the system in the first three days, for example, perhaps a call from a manager to explain why may be enough.

Case Study

Sage is a company known for its software; after all, software is its business. That doesn't mean, though, that they always knew Big Data or revenue marketing.[3] "We ... believed that we could communicate more effectively with our customers and prospects by speaking to them with one voice," said Nancy Harris, SVP and general manager at Sage. "We had been communicating with customers by product line and now we have the ability to be clearer and more consistent with our communications regarding the spectrum of offerings that Sage has for small- and medium-sized companies. Our goal is to make it easier for customers to determine which product best suits their needs and allow them to choose based on optimal fit."

Sage engaged The Pedowitz Group (or simply Pedowitz) who audited all of the company's marketing and technology. Pedowitz then scored

Sage's alignment between key areas of the company's operations and their technology (see Exhibit 9.4 for what these scores looked like after Sage implemented Pedowitz' recommendations). From this analysis came a set of recommendations designed to enable Sage to create what Pedowitz calls a Revenue Marketing Center of Excellence, including choosing marketing automation software. Harris says, though, "Building out a Revenue Marketing Center of Excellence can take from six months to three years. It's not an overnight journey. It's not something where you can get everyone in a room, align on a strategy, and knock it out in a couple of months. This takes a lot of hard work and a lot of deep thought around people, process, and technology to support what's best for the organization as a whole and ultimately, what will provide the best customer experience."

Several factors are important. First is the word *revenue*. From the beginning Harris and others at Sage were committed to the same goal: creating something that would deliver revenue. Whereas that is often the goal in a B2C world, that goal is tough for marketing in business to business. It meant that marketing could no longer simply focus on getting leads but getting leads that turned into sales and it meant that the sales force had to participate or that goal could not be accomplished.

A second factor is the word *journey*. Getting everyone on board is not an overnight job. By focusing on revenue, though, Harris and her team

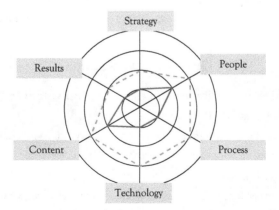

Exhibit 9.4. Sage's after action review sage, with help from the pedowitz group, measured their performance along these six dimensions following their implementation of a dynamic customer strategy approach to revenue generation. They perform much better in some areas, such as content and process, than others, such as strategy and results. This analysis provides insight for future direction.

had everyone's attention. And by delivering revenue, they were able to show increases of 25% in subscriptions and a 15% reduction in cold calling by salespeople, which significantly lowered the cost per opportunity.

None of that would have been possible, however, if the right business case hadn't been established up front. The focus on revenue and the recognition of the time needed meant that an accurate business case was established that documented the investment of time and energy needed *and* the return on that investment as well as the return on the financial investment.

Summary

Selecting a Big Data solution is much like any other capital budgeting problem. What makes it different is how you solve for challenges like determining the full return and comparing the future to the present when there are so many unknowns—even about the present. But making an effective business case requires creating an attractive vision for the future and documenting the path to get there, including the hard and soft costs and the hard and soft returns.

Big Data solutions also require somewhat unique approaches for measurement, like TTV, as well as for securing compliance. Managing change involving technology requires eliminating workarounds, involving users in design and implementation, and other tactics that can improve TTV.

Discussion Questions

1. Describe the implications of Paul Greenberg's statement "Value and values for value and values."
2. Discuss how resistance to change can slow TTV. What can you do before making a purchase that can help overcome resistance to change? Is lack of compliance only about resistance to change or are there other factors that can reduce compliance? If so, what are they?
3. Describe how you can improve TTV, based not just on this chapter but integrating what you've learned so far in this class and others.

CHAPTER 10

Customer Culture

The best CEOs I know are teachers, and at the core of what they teach is strategy.

—Michael Porter

Introduction

Over the past few chapters, models were simplified and operationalized into production systems. But once those models are launched, what comes next? The temptation is to let the models run and just cash the checks. Unfortunately, the world moves on and what worked yesterday may not work today. To gain that competitive advantage that comes from learning quicker and acting on that learning requires a customer knowledge competence (CKC), which is the subject of this chapter. As a Dynamic Customer Strategist, you should be able to:

- Identify the factors that support a CKC
- Create, build, and maintain a customer knowledge-driven culture
- Accelerate cycle time and learning
- Exploit the difference between strategic and tactical experimentation

In the usual book on strategy, the culminating chapter is a summary of the strategic plan, an outline of the document that represents the pinnacle of achievement based on the content of the book. But this is not the usual book. There is no strategy document, no final solution. By now, that material should already be familiar to you. Rather, we focus on how you lead an organization to a culture that engages Big Data, making the most of it through Dynamic Customer Strategy (DCS).

Leadership

There are literally hundreds of books on leadership. Some are modeled after great military or political leaders such as Patton; others on models such as Situational Leadership®. This is not one of those books. If you look at the quote, though, that starts this chapter, you begin to get a feel for the role that leadership plays in the development of a culture in which CKC using Big Data and DCS can flourish.

One of the promises we agreed to at the start of this book was that DCS provides a common language for communicating strategy. By creating your conceptual map of the market, terms are defined and important influencers of success are identified. A leader, then, should find the DCS map useful in teaching strategy—what's important for the firm's success, how success is measured, how and why factors are operationalized, and so forth.

Executive sponsorship has long been touted as a requirement for the successful application of Big Data. Having a leader say that building a competency based on customer knowledge is important for the company's success is a necessary condition for building that competency. But that isn't the same as mandating it. Recall an example from the previous chapter: The president of a business unit in a major global company decided that his unit would leverage customer relationship management (CRM) software so he ordered that it be purchased, that someone be hired to manage it, and so forth. Seven years later, he was long gone and the system was totally useless. Why? A mandate isn't enough. Salespeople never saw the value in the system so they didn't enter data properly. There was no single unified customer data because no one in other areas of the organization was willing to surrender ownership of their data.

What was lacking was agreement from all involved and that's because there was no leadership. There was no teaching of the strategy. There was no DCS map to guide the development of the processes by which the technology would be used or how people would be developed and their jobs transformed.

Contrast that with some of the organizations we've discussed throughout this book: Cabela's, Target, Royal Bank, Maybank, and others. These are companies where just about everyone catches the vision because leadership has taught the DCS map.

Customer Knowledge Competence

Big Data is data in motion—real-time data that helps the user antici-pate the future. Static data, the data that we've always used, can only tell us about history and frankly, the better we are at creating systems that describe history, the worse we become at anticipating the future.

But data in motion is only part of the story. The *company in motion* is what is really desired.

At the beginning of the book, we quoted Jack Welch. That quote is worth repeating: "The only sustainable competitive advantage is to be able to learn faster than your competition, and to be able to act on that learning." That quote essentially describes the purpose of creating **customer knowledge competence**, the organization's ability to acquire, analyze, disseminate, and operationalize customer information.

How does an organization build competence around customer knowl-edge? Clearly, Chapters 1 through 9 cover what is needed to build the competence. But what else is required?

CKC is a form of organizational competence, meaning that several factors are likely to be required for the competence to develop at the organizational level. First, the human resources have to be present, either through recruiting and selection processes and/or through training and development. In developing CKC, these resources have to be available for all steps, from information acquisition to application, though not neces-sarily in the same individual.

A second factor is the availability of tools needed to convert informa-tion into knowledge. These could include data warehousing technology, statistical software, and other tools, but could also include data acquisi-tion tools such as surveys, transaction data systems, web browsing data collection software, and the like. Similarly, there have to be tools that make knowledge available to the decision maker, such as through CRM systems, point-of-sale or point-of-interaction systems, service systems, and the like.

A third factor is the development of work processes and policies that support CKC. Reward systems should make CKC desirable, while work processes should make CKC possible. Having the ability to convert cus-tomer knowledge into intentions is insufficient; those intentions have to be turned into action for CKC to be realized.

Many modern-day technologists suggest that these characteristics can be boiled down to "people, process, and technology."[1] These alone, though, may not be enough. At least, simply buying the right people, processes (from a consultant), and technologies are only the foundation. Key to the entire process is the creation of a culture in which data skills and wins are celebrated, viewed as desirable, and become highly sought after. Organizations seeking a CKC must embrace a **customer culture** that supports this form of competence by valuing CKC, supporting it with the right reward system, and celebrating CKC as a vital component to the company's mission and strategy.

People

Finding, recruiting, selecting, and developing competent people is, in the general sense, a well-documented process. The challenge associated with the people dimension is that Big Data and CKC are not just based on one technology. Many critics and experts want to view Big Data as yet another innovation that will go through the standard adoption curve. But Big Data is more than a single innovation and CKC requires more than simply buying a technology. CKC is not based on a single tool. In truth, the effective use of Big Data requires more than skilled data scientists; it also requires strategists who understand how best to deploy the tool and tacticians who organize and manipulate data into operational models.

McKinsey Global Institute reported in 2011 that another 1.5 million data-capable business people are needed if businesses are to capitalize on

Factor	Description
Competent Individuals	Recruiting, selecting, and developing highly competent individuals capable of using the technology
Tools	Software, hardware, and other mechanisms for capturing data, analyzing it, and making knowledge available at the decision point
Processes & Policies	Work processes that take advantage of the knowledge and give the individual the flexibility to apply CKC to individual customer situations
Culture	CKC becomes part of the fabric of the organization, recognized as vital and celebrated as a key component of the organization's strategy

Exhibit 10.1. Factors influencing creation of a CKC.

Big Data.[2] If that estimation is accurate, then finding the people who can contribute to a CKC is not going to be easy.

Since this book is really about Big Data at the marketing interface, there are applications of Big Data that we've not discussed. Big Data also involves supply chain management, fraud detection, cash management— virtually every aspect of an organization can find applications of Big Data useful. What we've found in our research is that some companies are better at applying Big Data in some areas than others. Volvo, for example, is great at using Big Data in engineering safer cars but they're miserable at using Big Data to design more appealing cars. The point is that a company can develop competencies around Big Data but still not have a customer knowledge competency.

To really build a competency based on better use of customer data, intentionally seek out people with multiple skill-sets. As illustrated in Exhibit 10-2, a Customer Knowledge Competency (as opposed to Volvo's engineering competency) occurs when you successfully bring technology and statistics together with marketing. This means you have to seek out marketing people who understand either statistics or information technology, technologists who understand marketing, and statisticians who understand marketing.

Note that all must understand marketing. Maybe I'm over-emphasizing the point but a CKC requires that everyone understand the consumer.

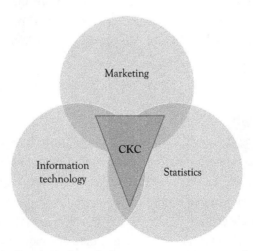

Exhibit 10.2. Customer knowledge competency requires functional competency in marketing, statistics, and information technology.

Just as importantly, the knowledge has to be as vertical in the organization as it is horizontal. In other words, management has to interact with data scientists. Starbucks is a great brand. But their CEO doesn't understand data and doesn't interact with data scientists.[3] Neither does the rest of the executive team. That's why they made those horrible blunders of over-expanded sites, over-expanded product categories, and other poor decisions. And whereas the current CEO may be effective at shrinking the company back to profitability, they aren't leveraging their customer data effectively because management can't be bothered to develop a comfort with customer data. They're competent, just not customer knowledge competent, and that will limit their ability to grow profitably.

Contrast that with Cabela's. Cabela's is a publicly-traded company, just as is Starbucks, but their board of directors regularly receives presentations from data scientists. Their board is as familiar with the company's customer personas as are the executives, merchants, and marketing staff. As a result, there is a culture that epitomizes the principles of DCS based on a Customer Knowledge Competency.

Although strategy and tactics are necessary components of an effective CKC, there are other people needed for other tasks. Yet, CKC involves many tools: statistics (of which predictive analytics is but one form), information technology (web, mobile, etc.), enterprise data warehousing, and marketing research (both qualitative and quantitative, which require different skill sets). Further, since CKC is neither just the acquisition of customer data nor the interpretation of that data but the integration of customer insight into decision making, process engineering is a necessary technology for effective CKC.

Tools

The tools necessary to CKC are more than just the technology associated with data. To be sure, an effective enterprise data warehouse (EDW) is necessary to make data available for analysis in real time. Yet, the information technology required is much broader.

An EDW that combines all customer data into one location is a minimum requirement. Having one version of the truth about your customers requires that you have consistent data definitions (recall Chapter 5) and that you have your data together in one place. If the data remain scattered all over the place, then data fiefdoms make analysis difficult and slow.

You are probably used to instant response from your computer. If a video takes more than a few seconds to download, you may multi-task and check your email. Big Data, however, can tie up massive computer systems for days—yes, days. An EDW does more than store data in one place; an effective data warehouse is one that makes data easy to retrieve. Although that sounds obvious, there are major differences in technologies. EDWs like those offered by Teradata are necessary to make the most of Big Data.

When I first met with Cabela's, they described a time before they got their Teradata EDW when it would take 6–8 hours to run fairly simple models. Retrieving the large data sets, formatting them for analysis, and actually conducting the analysis took hours. Some were longer than that and analysts would start the analysis before going home, hoping it would be ready in the morning. A few analyses actually took even longer, so these would be set to run over the weekend. Imagine the frustration when a glitch at 4 on a Sunday morning caused the system to crash and no one knew until 8 a.m. Monday. Whereas this scenario is now ancient history for Cabela's, it isn't for too many companies.

An important element is the sandbox. The **sandbox** is a portion of the EDW reserved for playing with the data, hence the term sandbox. A sample of the data is pulled out of the EDW and put into the sandbox for the duration of playtime. Now discovery can begin with the sample of the data without tying up the entire system. Why a sample of the data? Simply to shorten the process—a random sample of the data should still represent the population you are trying to study but a smaller data set is quicker to retrieve and quicker to analyze. Therefore, data scientists build their model in the sandbox, then apply it to the full data set once they're satisfied that the model is reasonably accurate. The final accuracy adjustments are made with the full data.

Other important tools include data visualization tools that improve reporting, drop-and-drag analytic tools like SAS or R, and the like. But these are all tools that enhance analytics.

Tools that link analytics to marketing operations are also needed. For example, mobile marketing tools need to link to customer databases.

HEB (a major grocery chain in Texas and Mexico), for example, can track your toilet paper purchases and know if you are nearly out of TP. If you are walking past the paper goods aisle and should be near the end of your TP inventory at home, HEB wants to push a reminder to you to stock up. That requires a mobile marketing tool in the store that is linked to their loyalty program, because it is the loyalty program that enables them to predict when you need TP. Thus, there are three tools needed: the customer database, the mobile marketing tool, and the tool that links these two together.

As you can see, creating a competency in customer knowledge requires a significant amount of technology. From what we've observed, the last to be considered is the linking tools. Companies find it easy to add marketing tools and marketing channels like proximity marketing tools. Proximity marketing (that is, pushing an offer to your phone while you're in the store) can occur without the use of customer data. For example, if the grocery store has a Rice Garden outlet in it, you could get an offer to stop in and take some Chinese food home. That doesn't require that the Rice Garden know whether you bought their food last time—no link to customer data is required. They could just push a coupon based on what isn't selling that day and begin generating a return.

But proximity marketing (and any marketing automation) works best when the device recognizes the customer. Then offers can be made that don't require giving up margin, or at least as much margin, and loyalty strengthened.

Imagine pulling into a Sonic (a drive-in fast food chain) and the person says, "Hi John, the usual?" Ok, maybe the scenario is not that unusual, but what if it was a Sonic location where you've never visited? If you are a loyal Sonic consumer, a customer database could recognize you and know what your usual is. That's the power of proximity marketing devices when there is a link between the customer database and the field system.

Thus, having the right tools means having the right technologies from home office to the field. The right hardware has to be served by the proper software, linked together and taking advantage of an EDW that can offer one complete and accurate view of the customer.

Process

Having the right people and the right tools isn't enough; creating the right culture also requires that processes support continually strengthening a competency built on customer knowledge. All processes—whether they be processes around managing people, managing supply, whatever—should support the creation and maintenance of a culture that puts customers first.

Research shows that how your people treat each other determines how they treat customers. If the purchasing department treats all areas of the company as customers and is concerned with their satisfaction, then the company is likely to have higher customer satisfaction. This relationship does not mean that the purchasing department has a direct effect on customer satisfaction; rather, it means that a customer-driven culture starts with treating all of your internal customers the right way. And that means that all processes have to be designed to serve customers, whether internal or external.

A second process characteristic of a customer culture is empowerment. Empowerment of employees to resolve challenges requires trust. Ritz-Carlton, the hotel chain with the highest customer satisfaction ratings among luxury hotels, once gave every employee a $1000 budget to resolve any customer issue without getting anyone's approval. No matter who—housekeeping, maintenance, front desk, didn't matter—they had up to $1000 to spend to take care of a customer without having to ask a manager for permission. After one year, no one had spent the money but customer satisfaction continued to climb.

Why? Because all they needed was permission to fix the problem as they and the customer saw fit and in every case, the resolution didn't require cash. Since then, some have had to spend money but the point isn't the money.

A third process characteristic of a DCS culture is that you build data systems for process improvement. If housekeepers are solving the same problem time after time, someone needs to fix whatever is causing the problem. That can't happen, though, unless data is captured and patterns in problems are identified and prioritized. Such data capture is easy if you have a customer service center where customer service reps are on the phone or chatting on the web with customers, not so easy if you are expecting housekeepers to enter the data.

Moreover, this data capture has to involve all processes, not just customer-serving processes. How many steps does it take your salespeople to get approval on a price or a proposal? How long does it take you to process a raise for an employee? In the first instance, those salespeople are someone's customers; in the second instance, you are someone's customer. Whoever is responsible for managing those processes should be monitoring those same processes with the right data to improve them.

Another characteristic of process improvement is time. When you have empowered people who have the right data, one output should be shorter processes. We already know the value of increased velocity when dealing with customers; the same value can be observed when increasing the velocity of internal processes that serve internal customers.

Accelerate Learning

Research into organizational learning over the past two decades has found that organizations with processes dedicated to learning have greater capacity for learning.[4] Although this relationship may seem obvious, the reality is that most organizations don't have the discipline it takes to focus on decision process improvement. Importantly, though, greater organizational capacity for learning is associated with higher levels of customer satisfaction.

Based on the research regarding organizational learning, there are several strategies you can take to create and support a culture of learning. The first is to be intentional about organizational learning. Since we already emphasize the importance of learning as a source for competitive advantage, being intentional about it is a foundation of all we've done so far. So let's take a closer look at the other actions you can take to create a culture of learning, summarized in Exhibit 10.3.

Whereas the old saw says "Great minds think alike," the reality is that if you hang around with the same people all the time, you all think alike and that doesn't mean great things occur. Organizations that intentionally combine people from different areas in informal ways are more likely to see organic innovation (that is, innovation created from within

- Intentionally co-mingle different functional areas to solve problems
- Brainstorm individually before brainstorming as a group
- Support team-based decision making
- Conduct after-action reviews of major decisions
- Create "scouts"

Exhibit 10.3. Tactics that accelerate organizational learning.

the organization, not acquired). When researchers trace the development of innovations, what they find is that it is in the weak links (relationships with acquaintances) of the innovator's social networks that ideas move.[5]

Cabela's, whether intentionally or not, does this by mingling members of the customer insights team with merchandising and marketing. By giving people short stints in other areas of the company, longer term benefits are derived from the understanding of that area that is created. The short-term benefits, though, include innovative solutions bred through diversity.

Of course, you can accomplish the same short-term objective by creating cross-functional teams. When faced with difficult challenges, sometimes bringing someone in from an area that doesn't seem to quite fit can actually spur great creativity.

Try this idea on for size in your next work group. Brainstorming is actually a poor strategy for learning. If you want to accelerate learning and innovation, ask for ideas from individuals. Then bring the group together and put all ideas up for discussion without revealing the source. Research shows you'll get more ideas and more creativity. Ideas occur because someone learns something. Accelerate learning by accelerating creativity.

Idea-generation should be individual; decision making should be team-based. Teams are better at choosing a course of action for a number of reasons, the most basic is that simply two (or 12) heads are better than one. But in groups, ideas get shot down or don't get put up to begin with, making groups weak for idea generation. Another reason for making decisions in groups is that you are more likely to have all of the people (or areas) involved that have to carry out the decision. That makes resistance less likely.

Another tactic, as illustrated in Exhibit 10.2, is the after-action review. In an after-action review, some of the questions you should consider are:

1. How long did the decision take? What could have been done to shorten that process—such as which approvals could have been skipped or delays avoided?
2. What information sources were used? Which ones contributed the most and the least? Why?
3. Does this decision need to be repeated regularly? If so, can it be made into a standard procedure or even automated?

This after-action review is reflective of a systems approach to learning. By developing stronger systems to support organizational learning, organizational capacity for learning is enhanced.

Finally, create scouts. **Scouts** are people assigned the task of scanning the horizon to find information that the organization needs.[6] For example, if an industry trade show is coming up, assign someone the role of gathering information on new technologies and products, whether the solutions are specifically in their job area or not. M&M Mars, the candy company, regularly sends plant and manufacturing engineers to trade shows in other industries looking for ideas that can be applied to candy making.

Case Study: Meredith Corporation

Meredith is probably not a familiar name to you, but you know their products. They publish magazines like *Better Homes & Gardens*, *Family Circle*, *Fitness*, *Successful Farming* and a lot more. You'd think that managing data for DCS purposes would be a natural when you have all of those subscriptions to manage. But up until about eleven years ago, all of that data was farmed out to a third party vendor because, well, the data weren't viewed as all that important.

The CEO, though, had a different vision for what the data could do and ordered it brought in-house. He also hired Antonio Lora, now Director of Enterprise Data Warehouse & Business Intelligence. When Antonio came on board, he quickly realized that there was a lot more than just technical challenges; the culture really wasn't ready to fully leverage data. Not only was the old outsourced process cumbersome and time consuming, it just caused managers to limit their perspective on what data could do, whether the data were trustworthy, and whether it was really worth the effort.

When Meredith insourced and installed their own Teradata enterprise data warehouse, data access went from days to hours and questions could be answered much more quickly. But if no one was asking the questions it didn't matter. So Lora developed and promoted an open access environment where managers were equipped to ask their own questions. For example, managers were given the opportunity to post their own reporting samples. Other managers could respond, tweaking the reports to provide stronger insight and voting on which ones to retain, which to drop. Not only did the number of reports being issued at least monthly go from 100 to 4000 (significantly increasing insight into the business), decision processes were strengthened as managers shared *with each other* why they wanted certain reports, how they intended to use those reports, and the nature of decisions they were making. The process also influenced data collection and data definition because now managers were demanding better data that provided a more complete picture.

But just wishing doesn't make it so. Managers still needed a lot of training and skills development in order to make the most of the tools, and this was not just training in how to operate the system. Educating on the value of data quality and collection is an ongoing process, especially given the nature of privacy policies in cooperative agreements with partners that make some data possible in some situations, impossible to retain in others.

As Lora says, "Building a data culture isn't ever a completed process. It's ongoing." Next up for Lora and Meredith Corp. is stronger analytical processes. As with the data, he'll have to manage this with limited resources, so it means analytical tools that the managers can use themselves. But as he says, "An environment of self-service means that managers really have to understand the value of data, trust the data, and know how to use it. And that makes from stronger managers and better decisions."

Exploiting Strategic Experimentation

A key component of DCS is experimentation. We've discussed the importance of multi-factorial designs to consider what works best, such as what price, which call to action, and the best communication frequency. These are, essentially, tactical questions.

At the beginning of the book, though, we discussed how strategy is theory in action. In addition to testing operational questions of call to action or messaging frequency, we also need to test the theoretical relationships. For example, how does satisfaction influence loyalty? I know— that question seems obvious but explain, then, why so many satisfied car buyers buy a different brand the next time around. The churn rate is greater than 50% among buyers who report being 95% satisfied!

If you are a car maker, you need to answer that question.

In every business, in every industry, there are important strategic questions like that requiring examination. Find the answer and you've got an important competitive advantage. *Not all learning is equal.*

The answer lies in creative use of Big Data coupled with DCS. Once the question is framed, then you can begin to explore those factors that are likely to influence the current outcome and the desired outcome. In our car example, the current outcome is low repurchase rate whereas the desired is a high repurchase rate, using a behavioral definition of loyalty. If satisfaction alone isn't driving repurchase, what is?

Executives for Buick decided, following market research and analysis of customer satisfaction data, that one important factor was styling—that the problem was that they hadn't kept up with style. Then using more research to iteratively design prospective models, significant improvements were reached. One result was the Enclave, a smashing success in spite of a 45% increase in price over the model it replaced.[7] Not only was the model attracting new buyers—after all, competitors were suffering from similar poor repurchase rates—it has already increased repurchase rates both from other Buick models and from Enclave to Enclave.

Summary

Big Data involves a wide array of technologies, but without the right people, processes, and tools, a Customer Knowledge Culture that wrings the most value from Big Data cannot be built. The technologies or tools include a single set of data definitions with data in an EDW, linkages between customer-facing systems and the EDW so that customer-level data can be applied, and other tools. But the right people have to be hired and developed into a culture that celebrates and supports a CKC, applying processes that make the most of the data that are available. Organizations must intentionally develop processes for higher velocity learning, and apply DCS to strategic questions to optimize competitive advantage.

Discussion Questions

1. You are looking for a job. How would you evaluate whether the company you are interviewing has a Customer Culture? That it has developed competence with customer knowledge?
2. How would your own personal professional development differ if you worked in a company with a customer culture? Be as specific as possible in contrasting your development against a company without such a culture.
3. What role does a leader play in the development of a customer culture? How does "the leader" differ from "leadership" in a customer culture?

Notes

Chapter 1

1. Philip Russom, director of TDWI Research, is generally credited with defining the three V characteristics of Big Data. Russom, Philip, (September 2011), *Big Data Analytics*, http://tdwi.org/research/2011/09/best-practices-report-q4-big-data-analytics.aspx
2. Molly McHugh (September 19, 2011). The Facebook effect hits the job market. *Digital Trends,* http://news.yahoo.com/facebook-effect-hits-job-market-005715783.html, accessed February 27, 2013.

Chapter 4

1. Lafley and Martin (2013).
2. Klingman and Tanner (2013).
3. Reichheld (2003), pp. 22–24.
4. The research supporting the effectiveness of a night's sleep on decision making is presented in a free e-book authored by sleep expert Maas (2013).
5. Domènech and Silvestre (2007).
6. The figure cited was reported by Bowes (2013), p. 5.
7. Kaye (2013).
8. This case study is based on Birkner (2013), pp. 38–45.

Chapter 5

1. Hipple (1988).

Chapter 6

1. Klingman and Tanner (2013).

Chapter 8

1. Kornhauser, Willensky, and Rand (2009), p. 1.

Chapter 9

1. Marketing (2012).
2. CBP Research (2013).
3. Qaqish (2013); Culbert, B.

Chapter 10

1. Wang (2011).
2. Manyika et al. (2011).
3. Kaye (2013), p. 24.
4. Hult (1998), pp. 193–216.
5. Ruef (2002), pp. 427–440.
6. Tanner and Drapeau (2013).
7. Borgias (2013).

References

Birkner, C. (2013, March 7). Marketing a best seller. *Marketing News*, pp. 38–45.

Borgias, B. (2013). *The power of design: Designing for experience*. Baylor Business.

Bosch–Domènech, A., & Silvestre, J. (2007). Averting risk in the face of large losses: Bernoulli vs. Tversky and Kahneman. *Economics Letters 107*(2), 180–182.

Bowes, P. (2013). *Position available: Data analytical talent unlocks business value for CEOs*. Retrieved April 4, 2013, from Pitney Bowers: http://news.pb.com/white-papers/position-available-data-analytical-talent-unlocks-business-value-for-ceos.htm

Buzz bit: Data-driven decisions (2013, March). *Marketing News*, p. 5.

CBP Research (2013). *The Case for a new CRM solution*. Retrieved from www.cbpresearch.com

Culbert, B. Retrieved from The Pedowitz Group: www.pedowitzgroup.com

Farris, P., Bendle, N., Pfeifer, P., & Reibstein, D. (2010). *Marketing metrics 2e: The definitive guide to measuring marketing performance*. Upper Saddle River, NJ: Pearson.

Hult, T. G. (1998). Managing the international strategic sourcing process as a market-driven organizational learning system. *Decision Sciences 29*(1), 193–216.

Kaye, K. (2013, March). At starbucks, data pours in. But what to do with it? *Ad Age*, p. 28.

Kaye, K. (2013, March). At starbucks, data pours in. But what to do with it? *Ad Age*, p. 24.

Klingman, P., & Tanner, J. F. (2013). *Creating a data-driven marketing culture*. Baylor Business Collaboratory Whitepaper #4-2013.

Klingman, P., & Tanner, J. F. (2013). *Data maturity in marketing decision-making: A study of retailers and consumer good manufacturers* (Report Number 1302). Baylor Business Collaboratory Research Report.

Kornhauser, D., Willensky, U., & Rand, W. (2009). Design guidelines for agent based model visualization *Journal of Artificial Societies and Social Simulation 12*(21), p.1. Retrieved August 14, 2008, from http://jasss.soc.surrey.ac.uk/12/2/1.html

Lafley, A. G., & Martin, R. L. (2013). *Playing to win: How strategy really works*. Boston, MA: Harvard Business Review Press.

Maas, J. (2013). *The power of sleep*. Retrieved on July 7, 2013, from Gallery Furniture: http://www.galleryfurniture.com/sleepcenter

Manyika et al. (2011). *Big data: The next frontier for innovation, competition, and productivity.* McKinsey Global Institute.

Marketing (2012, August). Big data: CMO set to outspend CIO on data-crunching technology. *Marketing Magazine.* www.marketingmagazine.com.

Molly, M. (2011). *The Facebook effect hits the job market.* Retrieved from September 19, 2011, from Digital Trends: http://news.yahoo.com/facebook-effect-hits-job-market-005715783.html

Philip, R. (2011). *Director of TDWI research, is generally credited with defining the three V characteristics of big data.* Retrieved September 2011, from Big Data Analytics: http://tdwi.org/research/2011/09/best-practices-report-q4-big-data-analytics.aspx

Qaqish, D. (2013). *The rise of the revenue marketer.* Alpharetta, GA: BookLogix.

Reichheld, F. (2003, December). One number you need to grow. *Harvard Business Review*, pp. 22–24.

Ruef, M. (2002). Strong ties, weak ties, and islands: Structural and cultural predictors of organizational innovation. *Industrial and Corporate Change 11*(3), 427–440.

Tanner, J. F., & Drapeau, N. (2013). *What attendees want in exhibitions* (Report AC-31). Center for Exhibition Industry Research.

Von Hipple. E. (1988) *The sources of innovation.* New York, NY: Oxford University Press.

Wang, K. (2013). *People, process technology management framework.* Retrieved on August 24, 2013, from: http://www.Kan-Wang.com

Index

OTHER TITLES IN OUR MARKETING STRATEGY COLLECTION

Naresh Malhotra, Georgia Tech, Editor

- *Decision Equity: The Ultimate Metric to Connect Marketing Actions to Profits* by Piyush Kumar
- *Building a Marketing Plan: A Complete Guide* by Ho Yin Wong
- *Top Market Strategy: Applying the 80/20 Rule* by Elizabeth Kruger
- *Pricing Segmentation and Analytics* by Tudor Bodea
- *Strategic Marketing Planning for the Small to Medium Sized Business: Writing a Marketing Plan* by David Anderson
- *Expanding Customer Service as a Profit Center Striving for Excellence and Competitive Advantage* by Rob Reider
- *Applying Scientific Reasoning to the Field of Marketing Make Better Decisions* by Terry Grapentine
- *Marketing Strategy for Small- to Medium-Sized Manufacturers: A Practical Guide for Generating Growth, Profit, and Sales* by Charles France
- *Basics of Branding: A Practical Guide for Managers* by Jay Gronlund
- *Marketing to the Bottom of the Pyramid: Text and Cases* by Ramendra Singh
- *Sustainable Consumption and Green Marketing* by Avinandan Mukherjee
- *Leading Edge Marketing: Turning Technology into Value* by Veronica Williams
- *Building Pricing Capabilities* by Manu Carricano

Announcing the Business Expert Press Digital Library

*Concise E-books Business Students Need
for Classroom and Research*

This book can also be purchased in an e-book collection by your library as
- a one-time purchase,
- that is owned forever,
- allows for simultaneous readers,
- has no restrictions on printing, and
- can be downloaded as PDFs from within the library community.

Our digital library collections are a great solution to beat the rising cost of textbooks. e-books can be loaded into their course management systems or onto student's e-book readers.

The **Business Expert Press** digital libraries are very affordable, with no obligation to buy in future years. For more information, please visit **www.businessexpertpress.com/librarians**. To set up a trial in the United States, please contact **Adam Chesler** at *adam.chesler@ businessexpertpress.com* for all other regions, contact **Nicole Lee** at *nicole.lee@igroupnet.com*.

www.ingramcontent.com/pod-product-compliance
Lightning Source LLC
Chambersburg PA
CBHW071158050326
40689CB00011B/2166

* 9 7 8 1 6 0 6 4 9 6 9 6 1 *